# 100 Research Topic Guides
## for Students

**Greenwood Professional Guides in School Librarianship**

School Library Media Centers in the 21st Century: Changes and Challenges
*Kathleen W. Craver*

Developing a Vision: Strategic Planning and the Library Media Specialist
*John D. Crowley*

Serving Special Needs Students in the School Library Media Center
*Caren L. Wesson and Margaret J. Keefe, editors*

Collaborations for Literacy: Creating an Integrated Language Arts Program
for Middle Schools
*Rochelle B. Senator*

How to Teach about American Indians: A Guide for the School Library
Media Specialist
*Karen D. Harvey with Lisa D. Harjo and Lynda Welborn*

# 100 Research Topic Guides
## for Students

## BARBARA WOOD BORNE

Greenwood Professional Guides in School Librarianship
*Harriet Selverstone, Series Adviser*

**GREENWOOD PRESS**
Westport, Connecticut • London

**Library of Congress Cataloging-in-Publication Data**

Borne, Barbara Wood.
    100 research topic guides for students / Barbara Wood Borne.
        p.   cm.—(Greenwood professional guides in school
    librarianship, ISSN 1074–150X)
    Includes bibliographical references and index.
    ISBN 0–313–29552–2 (alk. paper)
    1. Libraries—United States.   2. Searching, Bibliographical.
    3. Report writing.   I. Title.   II. Series.
    Z710.B73   1996
    025.5′2778223—dc20        95–42446

British Library Cataloguing in Publication Data is available.

Library of Congress Catalog Card Number: 95–42446
ISBN: 0–313–29552–2
ISSN: 1074–150X

First published in 1996

Greenwood Press, 88 Post Road West, Westport, CT  06881
An imprint of Greenwood Publishing Group, Inc.

Printed in the United States of America

The paper used in this book complies with the
Permanent Paper Standard issued by the National
Information Standards Organization (Z39.48–1984).

10 9 8 7 6 5 4

Dedicated to my favorite place in which to do research,
the Wallingford, Connecticut, Public Library

# Contents

# Introduction

"Where's the New Age section?"

"I've got to do a report on science. It can be *anything* relating to science."

"I have to write a paper on the Underground Railroad and I'm not allowed to use an encyclopedia. What else is there?"

"There's nothing on Bob Dylan in this library and I'm writing my junior essay on him. Help!"

"I noticed you don't have any books on quarks. I guess I should change my topic."

Because they are asked on a daily basis, these kinds of questions and comments will sound familiar to any librarian working with students. Of course, we are usually delighted when students choose to voice these concerns because then we can begin to introduce them to the variety of resources necessary to complete their assignments. Students who do not approach a librarian are often unable to locate the exact materials needed, or leave empty-handed. In these cases, everyone loses. The students feel the library failed them and the librarian missed an opportunity to provide a positive library experience for those students.

*100 Research Topic Guides for Students* was developed to help public librarians and school library media specialists to meet the needs of secondary school students seeking help with library research projects. Creatively presented or displayed, the guides in this book will be useful to the students who request assistance as well as to those who are hesitant to approach the reference desk.

Information in libraries today is available in many formats, including books, videotapes, audiocassettes, CDs, LPs, indexes, periodicals, pamphlets, printouts, online databases, CD-ROM databases, and microforms. Each of these formats could be subdivided as well, resulting in a seemingly endless variety of options for the library user.

Format is not the only variable in finding information. Location provides further challenges. Multiple sources of information are housed throughout the library building as well as in remote databases. All libraries have reference and circulating collections. Many have special collections, business areas, college and career centers, index tables, microform files, vertical files, consumer areas, atlas cases, foreign language materials, video collections, audiocassettes, CDs, and more. In addition, there may be a children's section and a young adult section in separate areas with their own materials and resources.

Technology introduces still another level of complexity in libraries today. Few libraries are untouched by the automation revolution, and most have bought into it in a big way. Card catalogs are increasingly online and often networked with other library systems. Databases, both online and CD-ROM, are installed in media centers or throughout the library. These public access catalogs and databases require searching techniques that vary from product to product.

Considering that information exists in multiple formats, locations, and databases, the library could appear user unfriendly to the student walking in with an assignment to write a research paper on acid rain or to prepare a debate topic advocating the death penalty.

Our challenge and mission as librarians is to integrate the needs of students with the nature of the library. The Resource Topic Guides in this book are designed as pathfinders to acquaint students with some of the resources available on a particular topic in various formats throughout the library. By introducing students to the access points appropriate for their information search, the Guides help students to find what they need and to discover that they can use the library successfully. This will provide the positive reinforcement necessary to encourage continued use of the library.

# How to Use This Book

*100 Research Topic Guides for Students* was developed to facilitate a smooth interface between the student and the library, to reduce the level of frustration often encountered when students try to locate information without understanding the system, and to encourage in-depth use of the library that will help to ensure successful results. With the use of a Research Topic Guide, the student is introduced to the library in microcosm and is exposed to the full scope of possible materials to be tapped. Each Guide serves not only as a map to library resources but as an outline to library research procedures.

Students coming to the library to do research have varying needs. Some have a research project to do but have not yet selected a topic. Others have been assigned a specific topic and need resources to obtain information on that topic. Some from the latter group will need to refine or narrow the scope of their chosen topic.

## RESEARCH TOPIC GUIDE FORMAT AND RATIONALE

An understanding of the format and intent of the Research Topic Guides is necessary for the librarian to effectively assist the student in their use. Following is a brief analysis of each section, with comments as to rationale.

### Topic

Although student assignments vary considerably within subject area and grade level, there is a recognizable pattern to assignments, as all experienced librarians know. This pattern corresponds to local curriculum requirements, perennially favorite teacher topics, the special interests of teenagers, and current hot issues. *100 Research Topic Guides for Students* contains topics selected to meet the above criteria. Research Topic Guides are grouped into four main subject areas: science and technology, social issues, social studies, and biography. Topics range from the frequently assigned (Abortion, AIDS, Earthquakes, and Civil Rights) to the unusual but popular (Nostradamus, Woodstock, John Lennon, and DNA Fingerprinting). Many topics are broad, such as Oceanography and the Holocaust, because this is often the way the student perceives the assignment. The Research Topic Guide can help the student narrow the topic, however. Other topics are more specific, for example, Quarks, Legal Rights of Teenagers, and Generation X. Students who have some flexibility or who have not yet chosen a subject can select from this group. These, too, can be further narrowed to achieve an effective focus.

Many topics covered reflect the interests of teenagers; such topics include Jimi Hendrix, New Age Movement, and Witchcraft Trials. Yet these ideas rarely occur to students with open-ended research assignments. By browsing through these diverse Research Topic Guides, students may consider choosing a topic with personal meaning and realize that their own interests provide valid research subjects. Certain topics were selected for this book because of their appeal to teenagers combined with the relative difficulty in discovering information on them. With a Research Topic Guide on V. C. Andrews or Woodstock, students can find success locating information that might otherwise be hard to find.

### Background

Background information is included to provide the student with a brief overview of the subject to help with selection.

### Browse for Books on the Shelf Using These Call Numbers

The Dewey decimal classification system is used because it is standard for most school media centers and public libraries. Selective browsing is an effective method for retrieving materials on a particular subject. The call numbers, represented individually or as a range, generally appear in order of descending importance. Remember that catalogers and libraries differ considerably in assigning call numbers so this is only a list of suggested areas in which to look for material on a particular subject.

### Look under the Following Subjects in the Catalog (Card or Computer)

Library of Congress subject headings are used in this section because they are standard in most school media centers and public libraries. The selection of particular headings varies among catalogers and libraries. Those included in this section tend to be regularly assigned to the topic, generally appear in order of descending importance, and serve as suggestions.

### Use Pamphlet File (Also Called Vertical File) under the Headings

This section is included only if school media centers and public libraries would include the topic in a pamphlet file.

### Reference Materials That May Help (Books or CD-ROMs)

Specific reference sources pertaining to the topic and general reference works that include information on the topic are listed here. Occasionally these sources are also available on CD-ROM, though no designation as to format is indicated. Reference periodicals that cover topics on a regular basis are listed without dates, such as *Background Notes*, *Congressional Quarterly Weekly Report*, *Editorials on File*, *Facts on File*, and *Today's Science on File*.

### Periodical Indexes to Search (Books or CD-ROMs)

Indexes included may be available in book and/or CD-ROM depending on the nature of the product and the particular library. Suggested indexes represent those commonly found in school media centers and public libraries and are not intended to be a comprehensive listing.

### Online Databases to Search

Although there is tremendous variation in online searching capabilities among libraries, it is clear that the trend toward providing this service will continue to grow. Some libraries require that the search be performed by a librarian, some allow students to do their own online searching, and many students can access online sources from their home systems. Even within a single library, searching online systems can vary from product to product. Internet stations may be provided to the public, while Dialog searching is done by professional staff. Online public access computers may allow the student to search a variety of databases.

This section includes a listing of several online products that may be useful in locating information on the topic. Because the Internet and other online resources are constantly changing and evolving, no attempt has been made to indicate a specific database or file to search. Many students will need assistance both in selecting a specific source and in learning searching techniques. (See Appendix C—Guide to Searching Databases.) The reference interview is an appropriate forum to deal with these issues.

### Key Words and Descriptors for Periodical Index and Online Searches

Included here are key words and descriptors useful for searching periodical indexes (book or CD-ROM) and online databases. Since no two products are searched in the same way or require the identical descriptors, flexibility is required. Using the list provided, students will retrieve material successfully and can expand their search as needed. Key words and descriptors generally appear in order of descending importance.

### Videotapes on This Topic

Videotapes listed here are generally appropriate for secondary school students and relate in some way to the topic. Since availability will vary widely among libraries, students should be reminded to check the holdings of their own library to locate additional videotapes.

### Fiction Books Relating to Topic

Titles included in this section are generally appropriate for secondary school students and should be easily obtainable in most libraries or through interlibrary loan. Occasionally, when young adult fiction on a topic is not available, adult titles are listed and identified as such. If there are no works of fiction on a particular topic, the section is omitted.

### National Organizations to Contact for Additional Information

National sources of information are included for students who wish to pursue their search for information outside the library. Whenever possible, organizations were chosen based on one or more of the following criteria: a stated intent to provide information to the public, national prominence, and representation of differing viewpoints.

If appropriate organizations are not available for a particular topic, this section is omitted.

### Suggestions for Narrowing This Topic

Suggestions for narrowing the topic are included here to help students refine their subject. These ideas represent only a few of the possibilities. Brainstorming among students and friends or between the student and the librarian or teacher will result in other options. The intent is to encourage students to take time to focus on one aspect of their topic before plunging into the research process. Suggested topics are not prioritized but listed in alphabetical order.

### Suggestions for Related Topics

Included in this section are separate and distinct subjects related in some respect to the topic. If the student is permitted leeway in choosing a research topic, he or she may find something of interest in this list of ideas. These suggested subjects may be broad or narrow and represent only a few of the many possible related topics; they are listed in alphabetical order.

### Disclaimer

A disclaimer is appended to the end of each Research Topic Guide stating that resources on the topic include, but are not limited to, those listed. Also, as indicated, students are encouraged to request help from a librarian. A Research Topic Guide cannot replace a librarian and the important interaction of the reference interview. However, student and librarian together using the Guide can successfully navigate the library research process.

## USING RESEARCH TOPIC GUIDES IN YOUR LIBRARY

### Adapting Research Topic Guides

The Research Topic Guides in this book are designed to be generic and therefore applicable in as many libraries and school media centers as possible. Photocopying Research Topic Guides for easy, convenient distribution is recommended. They can be taken directly from the book and used in their current form. However, librarians with the time and interest are encouraged to personalize Research Topic Guides to correspond with the collections of their individual libraries. Sections appropriate for adaptation are (1) Reference Materials That May Help, (2) Periodical Indexes to Search, (3) Online Databases to Search, (4) Videotapes on This Topic, and (5) Fiction Books Relating to Topic. The availability of these specific resources will vary. A page listing local resource materials could easily be developed and attached to each Research Topic Guide as it is given to a student.

### Promoting Research Topic Guides

Options for promoting the use of Research Topic Guides to students will vary among libraries. A small section of the reference desk or a nearby table or homework center could be devoted to a "Hot Report Topics" or "Current Assignment Ideas" display. The book could be featured to allow for browsing by students.

Another approach would involve photocopying a variety of Research Topic Guides for distribution to students. These could be placed in labeled folders in a similar display arrangement. Students could select topics from the folders or use the book for additional suggestions.

In addition to aids for researching specific topics, Research Topic Guides can serve as templates for creating new worksheets on additional topics. Students may wish to pursue topics not covered or choose from the related topics listed on each Guide. By following the Research Topic Guide format, these students can create their own guides to research. A blank form for this purpose is included in the Appendixes.

### Aids to Research

In addition to using the Research Topic Guides, students may need help in negotiating the research process. To that end, the following aids to research are included in the Appendixes: Note-Taking Procedures, Bibliographic Citation Format, and Database Searching Techniques. These guidelines can be photocopied and distributed to students to use in conjunction with the Research Topic Guides.

### NOTE

The publisher grants permission to the reader to photocopy individual topic guides for research purposes.

# I

# Science and Technology
# Research Topic Guides

# Acid Rain

**BACKGROUND**

Acid rain, a form of pollution caused by the combination of nitrogen dioxide, sulfur, and atmospheric moisture, can occur as rain, snow, hail, or fog. Scientists agree that acid rain damages the environment, but they disagree as to the severity of the problem.

**BROWSE FOR BOOKS ON THE SHELF USING THESE CALL NUMBERS**

> 363.7–363.7394
> 333.91

**LOOK UNDER THE FOLLOWING SUBJECTS IN THE CATALOG (CARD OR COMPUTER)**

> Acid rain
> Acid rain—Environmental aspects
> Acid rain—Environmental aspects—United States
> Acid rain—Experiments
> Acid rain—Laws and regulations
> Pollution

**USE PAMPHLET FILE (ALSO CALLED VERTICAL FILE) UNDER THE HEADINGS**

> Acid rain
> Pollution

**REFERENCE MATERIALS THAT MAY HELP (BOOKS OR CD-ROMS)**

> *CQ Researcher*, March 3, 1991.
> *Editorials on File*. Facts on File.
> *Facts on File*
> *McGraw-Hill Encyclopedia of Science and Technology*, 1992.
> *The New Book of Popular Science*. Grolier, 1994.
> General encyclopedias

**PERIODICAL INDEXES TO SEARCH (BOOKS OR CD-ROMS)**

> EBSCO Magazine Article Summaries
> InfoTrac
> NewsBank and other newspaper indexes
> Readers' Guide to Periodical Literature
> SIRS (Social Issues Resources Series)
> WILSONDISC

## ONLINE DATABASES TO SEARCH

America Online
CompuServe
Dialog
Internet
Prodigy

## KEY WORDS AND DESCRIPTORS FOR PERIODICAL INDEX AND ONLINE SEARCHES

Acid rain
Acid precipitation

## VIDEOTAPES ON THIS TOPIC

*Acid Rain: New Bad News*. Ambrose Video, 1985.
*Acid Rain*. Schlessinger Video Productions, 1993.

## NATIONAL ORGANIZATIONS TO CONTACT FOR ADDITIONAL INFORMATION

Acid Rain Foundation, 1410 Varsity Dr., Raleigh, NC 27606–2010.
Center for Clean Air Policy, 444 N. Capitol St., Ste. 602, Washington, DC 20001.

## SUGGESTIONS FOR NARROWING THIS TOPIC

Effects of acid rain on cities, forests, soil, water, wildlife, crops, or humans
Fog
Haze
Clean Air Act of 1990

## SUGGESTIONS FOR RELATED TOPICS

Air pollution
Global warming
Greenhouse effect
Oceanography
Rain forests

This RESEARCH TOPIC GUIDE is intended to help the library user find information and materials on a particular topic in many sources throughout the library. Resources on this topic are not limited to those described and availability will depend upon the individual library. Feel free to ask a librarian for assistance.

# Alternative Medicine

## BACKGROUND

Although much about it still remains unknown, alternative medicine is acknowledged as having some success in treating certain medical disorders. Innovative practices under the banner of alternative medicine include chiropractic, acupuncture, homeopathy, and naturopathy. Many in the medical profession refute the value of alternative medicine, whereas some professionals feel it has a place. Debate on the topic continues.

## BROWSE FOR BOOKS ON THE SHELF USING THESE CALL NUMBERS

615.5–615.53
615.851
133
610

## LOOK UNDER THE FOLLOWING SUBJECTS IN THE CATALOG (CARD OR COMPUTER)

Alternative medicine
Holistic medicine
Naturopathy

## REFERENCE MATERIALS THAT MAY HELP (BOOKS OR CD-ROMS)

Burroughs, Hugh, and Mark Kastner. *Alternative Healing: The Complete A–Z Guide to over 160 Different Alternative Therapies*, 1993.
*CQ Researcher*, January 31, 1992.
*McGraw-Hill Encyclopedia of Science and Technology*, 1992.
General encyclopedias

## PERIODICAL INDEXES TO SEARCH (BOOKS OR CD-ROMS)

EBSCO Magazine Article Summaries
InfoTrac
NewsBank and other newspaper indexes
Readers' Guide to Periodical Literature
SIRS (Social Issues Resources Series)
WILSONDISC

## ONLINE DATABASES TO SEARCH

America Online
CompuServe
Dialog

Internet

Prodigy

## KEY WORDS AND DESCRIPTORS FOR PERIODICAL INDEX AND ONLINE SEARCHES

Alternative medicine

Holistic medicine

Naturopathy

Folk medicine

## VIDEOTAPES ON THIS TOPIC

*Healing and the Mind.* Ambrose Video, 1993.

*Powerful Medicine.* Films, Inc., 1986.

## FICTION BOOK RELATING TO TOPIC

Dickinson, Peter. *Healer*, 1987.

## NATIONAL ORGANIZATIONS TO CONTACT FOR ADDITIONAL INFORMATION

American Holistic Medical Association, 4101 Lake Boone Trail, Ste. 201, Raleigh, NC 27607.

National Institutes of Health, Office of Alternative Medicine, 9000 Rockville Pike, Bldg. 1, No. 126, Bethesda, MD 20892.

## SUGGESTIONS FOR NARROWING THIS TOPIC

Discuss the role of the mind in healing.

Highlight the history of alternative medicine.

Present the case for (or against) alternative medicine.

Choose a specific type of alternative medicine to research; e.g., acupuncture, aroma therapy, laugh therapy, herbal medicine.

## SUGGESTIONS FOR RELATED TOPICS

Eastern medicine

Faith healers

Folk medicine

Macrobiotics

Yoga

This RESEARCH TOPIC GUIDE is intended to help the library user find information and materials on a particular topic in many sources throughout the library. Resources on this topic are not limited to those described and availability will depend upon the individual library. Feel free to ask a librarian for assistance.

# DNA Fingerprinting

**BACKGROUND**

First used as evidence in a U.S. court in a 1988 Florida rape trial, DNA fingerprinting is a laboratory technique that compares the unique genetic structure of a person's blood to that of tissue samples found at a crime scene; a match would indicate guilt. Use of scientific evidence in court proceedings has become more common but continues to be a topic of controversy.

**BROWSE FOR BOOKS ON THE SHELF USING THESE CALL NUMBERS**

> 364.1523
> 614.1

**LOOK UNDER THE FOLLOWING SUBJECTS IN THE CATALOG (CARD OR COMPUTER)**

> DNA fingerprinting
> DNA fingerprints
> DNA—Genetics
> Forensic medicine

**USE PAMPHLET FILE (ALSO CALLED VERTICAL FILE) UNDER THE HEADING**

> Genetics

**REFERENCE MATERIALS THAT MAY HELP (BOOKS OR CD-ROMS)**

> *CQ Researcher*, October 22, 1993.
> Magill, Frank N., ed. *Great Events from History II: Science and Technology Series*, 1991.
> *McGraw-Hill Encyclopedia of Science and Technology*, 1992.
> *The New Book of Popular Science*. Grolier, 1994.
> *Today's Science on File*. Facts on File.
> General encyclopedias

**PERIODICAL INDEXES TO SEARCH (BOOKS OR CD-ROMS)**

> EBSCO Magazine Article Summaries
> InfoTrac
> NewsBank and other newspaper indexes
> Readers' Guide to Periodical Literature
> SIRS (Social Issues Resources Series)
> WILSONDISC

## ONLINE DATABASES TO SEARCH

America Online
CompuServe
Dialog
Internet
Prodigy

## KEY WORDS AND DESCRIPTORS FOR PERIODICAL INDEX AND ONLINE SEARCHES

DNA analysis
DNA fingerprints
Forensic medicine
Law enforcement technology

## VIDEOTAPE ON THIS TOPIC

*DNA Databases: Forensic Use vs. Potential for Private Abuse.* Video Library Project, 1993.

## FICTION BOOK RELATING TO TOPIC

Wambaugh, Joseph. *The Blooding*, 1989. (adult)

## NATIONAL ORGANIZATIONS TO CONTACT FOR ADDITIONAL INFORMATION

Milton Helpern Institute of Forensic Medicine, 520 First Ave., New York, NY 10016.
National Institute for Citizen Education in the Law, 711 G St., S.E., Washington, DC 20003–2861.

## SUGGESTIONS FOR NARROWING THIS TOPIC

Consider the use of DNA fingerprinting in historical research or wildlife research.
Discuss the moral and ethical aspects of DNA fingerprinting evidence in the courtroom.
Examine the national DNA databank and the privacy issue.
Research a specific case in which DNA fingerprinting was used to solve a crime.

## SUGGESTIONS FOR RELATED TOPICS

Civil liberty and forensic medicine
Forensic medicine
Genetic engineering
Medical ethics
Polygraph testing
Scientific evidence in court

This RESEARCH TOPIC GUIDE is intended to help the library user find information and materials on a particular topic in many sources throughout the library. Resources on this topic are not limited to those described and availability will depend upon the individual library. Feel free to ask a librarian for assistance.

# Earthquakes

## BACKGROUND

An earthquake is a natural phenomenon caused by seismic (sound) waves transmitted through the earth and causing the surface of the earth to tremble for a varying period of time. The degree of shaking can range from nearly undetectable to violent and devastating.

## BROWSE FOR BOOKS ON THE SHELF USING THESE CALL NUMBERS

551.2–551.29
551.59

## LOOK UNDER THE FOLLOWING SUBJECTS IN THE CATALOG (CARD OR COMPUTER)

Earthquakes
Earthquakes—California
Earthquake prediction
Seismology

## USE PAMPHLET FILE (ALSO CALLED VERTICAL FILE) UNDER THE HEADING

Earthquakes

## REFERENCE MATERIALS THAT MAY HELP

*CQ Researcher*, December 16, 1994.
Magill, Frank N., ed. *Magill's Survey of Science: Earth Science Series*, 1990.
*McGraw-Hill Encyclopedia of Science and Technology*, 1992.
*The New Book of Popular Science*. Grolier, 1992.
Ritchie, David. *The Encyclopedia of Earthquakes and Volcanoes*, 1994.
General encyclopedias

## PERIODICAL INDEXES TO SEARCH (BOOKS OR CD-ROMS)

EBSCO Magazine Article Summaries
InfoTrac
NewsBank and other newspaper indexes
Readers' Guide to Periodical Literature
SIRS (Social Issues Resources Series)
WILSONDISC

## ONLINE DATABASES TO SEARCH

America Online
CompuServe
Dialog
Internet
Prodigy

## KEY WORDS AND DESCRIPTORS FOR PERIODICAL INDEX AND ONLINE SEARCHES

Earthquakes
Choose a specific earthquake as a key word; e.g., Loma Prieta.
Seismology
Seismic waves
Earthquake prediction

## VIDEOTAPES ON THIS TOPIC

*Earthquake*. Vestron Video, 1992.
*Predictable Disaster*. Vestron Video, 1989.

## FICTION BOOKS RELATING TO TOPIC

Bethancourt, T. E. *The Tomorrow Connection*, 1984.
Gregory, Kristiana. *Earthquake at Dawn*, 1992.
Gray, Genevieve S. *Alaska Woman*, 1977.

## NATIONAL ORGANIZATION TO CONTACT FOR ADDITIONAL INFORMATION

Earthquake Engineering Research Institute, 499 14th St., Ste. 320, Oakland, CA 94612–1902.

## SUGGESTIONS FOR NARROWING THIS TOPIC

Choose a specific earthquake to research; e.g., Armenian earthquake of 1988, Northridge, California earthquake of 1994, or the San Francisco earthquake of 1906.
Discuss the psychological effects of earthquakes on people.
Investigate the science of earthquake predicting.
What is the San Andreas Fault?

## SUGGESTIONS FOR RELATED TOPICS

Kourion (extinct city)
Plate Tectonics
Richter Scale
Tsunamis (tidal waves)
Volcanoes

This RESEARCH TOPIC GUIDE is intended to help the library user find information and materials on a particular topic in many sources throughout the library. Resources on this topic are not limited to those described and availability will depend upon the individual library. Feel free to ask a librarian for assistance.

# Electromagnetic Fields (EMFs)—Health Aspects

## BACKGROUND

Electromagnetic fields (EMFs) occur when electricity is utilized and conducted. Electromagnetic radiation is produced by the combination of these electric and magnetic forces. EMFs occur everywhere in our environment: electric blankets, toasters, microwaves, cellular phones, power lines, and so on. In the last decade some researchers have attempted to link exposure to EMFs to a higher frequency of cancer occurrences. Research is ongoing and there is much debate on this topic.

## BROWSE FOR BOOKS ON THE SHELF USING THIS CALL NUMBER

363.189

## LOOK UNDER THE FOLLOWING SUBJECTS IN THE CATALOG (CARD OR COMPUTER)

Electromagnetic fields—Health aspects
Electric lines—Health aspects
Electromagnetic radiation

## REFERENCE MATERIALS THAT MAY HELP

*CQ Researcher*, October 22, 1993.
*McGraw-Hill Encyclopedia of Science and Technology*, 1992.
*The New Book of Popular Science*. Grolier, 1994.
*Science and Technology Desk Reference*. Gale, 1993.
*Today's Science on File*. Facts on File.
General encyclopedias

## PERIODICAL INDEXES TO SEARCH (BOOKS OR CD-ROMS)

EBSCO Magazine Article Summaries
InfoTrac
NewsBank and other newspaper indexes
Readers' Guide to Periodical Literature
SIRS (Social Issues Resources Series)
WILSONDISC

## ONLINE DATABASES TO SEARCH

America Online
CompuServe
Dialog

Internet
Prodigy

## KEY WORDS AND DESCRIPTORS FOR PERIODICAL INDEX AND ONLINE SEARCHES

Electromagnetic radiation
Electromagnetic waves
Electric lines
EMFs
EMFs and cancer

## NATIONAL ORGANIZATIONS TO CONTACT FOR ADDITIONAL INFORMATION

Bio-Electro-Magnetics Institute, 2490 W. Moana Lane, Reno, NV 89509–3936.
Electric Power Research Institute, 3412 Hillview Ave., Palo Alto, CA 94304.

## SUGGESTIONS FOR NARROWING THIS TOPIC

Investigate the possible link between EMFs and cancer.
Present a scientific discussion of EMFs.
Research the degree of low-level radiation emitted by various appliances.

## SUGGESTIONS FOR RELATED TOPICS

Chernobyl Nuclear Power Station disaster
Health aspects relating to video display terminals
Radon
X-ray technology

This RESEARCH TOPIC GUIDE is intended to help the library user find information and materials on a particular topic in many sources throughout the library. Resources on this topic are not limited to those described and availability will depend upon the individual library. Feel free to ask a librarian for assistance.

# Genetic Engineering

## BACKGROUND

Genetic engineering involves the practice of altering the genetic structure of living cells for the purpose of curing disease and improving the quality of life. Because both positive and potentially negative results could occur from genetic manipulation, it has become a controversial topic. Experts in the fields of medicine, religion, and philosophy as well as concerned people everywhere are struggling with this vital issue.

## BROWSE FOR BOOKS ON THE SHELF USING THESE CALL NUMBERS

> 660.65
> 616.042
> 573.2
> 575.1
> 301.423

## LOOK UNDER THE FOLLOWING SUBJECTS IN THE CATALOG (CARD OR COMPUTER)

> Genetic engineering
> Genetic engineering—Social aspects
> Biotechnology
> Medical genetics

## USE PAMPHLET FILE (ALSO CALLED VERTICAL FILE) UNDER THE HEADINGS

> Genetic engineering
> Biotechnology

## REFERENCE MATERIALS THAT MAY HELP (BOOKS OR CD-ROMS)

> *CQ Researcher*, October 18, 1991; August 5, 1994; April 8, 1994.
> *Editorials on File*. Facts on File.
> *Facts on File*
> *McGraw-Hill Encyclopedia of Science and Technology*, 1992.
> *The New Book of Popular Science*. Grolier, 1994.
> *Science and Technology Desk Reference*. Gale, 1993.
> *Today's Science on File*. Facts on File.

## PERIODICAL INDEXES TO SEARCH (BOOKS OR CD-ROMS)

> EBSCO Magazine Article Summaries
> Readers' Guide to Periodical Literature
> InfoTrac
> NewsBank and other newspaper indexes
> SIRS (Social Issues Resources Series)
> WILSONDISC

## ONLINE DATABASES TO SEARCH

America Online
CompuServe
Dialog
Internet
Prodigy

## KEY WORDS AND DESCRIPTORS FOR PERIODICAL INDEX AND ONLINE SEARCHES

Genetic engineering
Genetic research
Biotechnology
Gene therapy

## VIDEOTAPES ON THIS TOPIC

*Genetic Engineering: The Nature of Change*. Monsanto, 1986.
*The Infinite Voyage: The Geometry of Life*. Vestron Video, 1988.
*Jurassic Park*. MCA Universal Home Video, 1994.

## FICTION BOOKS RELATING TO TOPIC

Crichton, Michael. *Jurassic Park*, 1990.
McCaffrey, Anne. *Powers That Be*, 1993.
Sanders, Scott R. *The Engineer of Beasts*, 1992.

## NATIONAL ORGANIZATION TO CONTACT FOR ADDITIONAL INFORMATION

Genetics Society of America, 9650 Rockville Pike, Bethesda, MD 20814–3998.

## SUGGESTIONS FOR NARROWING THIS TOPIC

Analyze the dangers of genetic engineering.
Comment on in vitro fertilization.
Discuss the ethical aspects of cloning, gene therapy, or sex preselection.
Investigate the benefits of genetic engineering.

## SUGGESTIONS FOR RELATED TOPICS

Biological warfare
DNA fingerprinting
Eugenics
Fertility treatments
Surrogate mothers

This RESEARCH TOPIC GUIDE is intended to help the library user find information and materials on a particular topic in many sources throughout the library. Resources on this topic are not limited to those described and availability will depend upon the individual library. Feel free to ask a librarian for assistance.

# Greenhouse Effect

## BACKGROUND

The greenhouse effect is a term used by scientists to describe the way gases in the earth's lower atmosphere trap infrared radiation (heat) emanating from the earth's surface. This phenomenon is similar to the way a greenhouse traps and holds heat. Scientists are concerned that pollution and other environmental changes may cause the temperature of the earth's surface to increase, resulting in the melting of the polar icecap, a rise in sea level, and other environmental dangers.

## BROWSE FOR BOOKS ON THE SHELF USING THESE CALL NUMBERS

363.7–363.7392
551.6

## LOOK UNDER THE FOLLOWING SUBJECTS IN THE CATALOG (CARD OR COMPUTER)

Greenhouse effect, Atmospheric
Global warming
Climatic changes
Pollution

## USE PAMPHLET FILE (ALSO CALLED VERTICAL FILE) UNDER THE HEADINGS

Greenhouse effect, Atmospheric
Global warming
Ozone layer depletion
Air pollution

## REFERENCE MATERIALS THAT MAY HELP (BOOKS OR CD-ROMS)

*Facts on File*
*McGraw-Hill Encyclopedia of Science and Technology*, 1992.
*The New Book of Popular Science*, Grolier, 1994.
*Today's Science on File*. Facts on File.
General encyclopedias

## PERIODICAL INDEXES TO SEARCH (BOOKS OR CD-ROMS)

EBSCO Magazine Article Summaries
InfoTrac
NewsBank and other newspaper indexes
Readers' Guide to Periodical Literature
SIRS (Social Issues Resources Series)
WILSONDISC

## ONLINE DATABASES TO SEARCH

America Online
CompuServe
Dialog
Internet
Prodigy

## KEY WORDS AND DESCRIPTORS FOR PERIODICAL INDEX AND ONLINE SEARCHES

Greenhouse effect
Global warming
Climatic changes

## VIDEOTAPES ON THIS TOPIC

*Global Environment*. PBS Video, 1988.
*Spaceship Earth: Our Global Environment*. Worldlink, 1991.

## FICTION BOOK RELATING TO TOPIC

Llywelyn, Morgan. *The Elementals*, 1993.

## NATIONAL ORGANIZATIONS TO CONTACT FOR ADDITIONAL INFORMATION

Greenhouse Action, P.O. Box 16743, Seattle, WA 98116–0743.
Greenhouse Crisis Foundation, 1130 17th St., N.W., Ste. 630, Washington, DC 20036.
National Science Foundation, 1800 G. St., N.W., Rm. 520, Washington, DC 20550.

## SUGGESTIONS FOR NARROWING THIS TOPIC

Describe the impact of trees and forests on the greenhouse effect.
Discuss international efforts to reduce the greenhouse effect.
Examine how the greenhouse effect impacts sea level, the ozone layer, and/or plant life.

## SUGGESTIONS FOR RELATED TOPICS

Acid rain
Desertification
Earth Summit in Rio de Janeiro, 1992
Gaia
Volcanoes

This RESEARCH TOPIC GUIDE is intended to help the library user find information and materials on a particular topic in many sources throughout the library. Resources on this topic are not limited to those described and availability will depend upon the individual library. Feel free to ask a librarian for assistance.

# Hazardous Wastes

**BACKGROUND**

Federal law defines waste as hazardous if it corrodes, explodes, ignites easily, reacts with water, is unstable when heated, or is poisonous. Issues in hazardous waste management involve the effects and disposal of these environmental pollutants and health hazards.

**BROWSE FOR BOOKS ON THE SHELF USING THESE CALL NUMBERS**

>   363.729
>   363.7392

**LOOK UNDER THE FOLLOWING SUBJECTS IN THE CATALOG (CARD OR COMPUTER)**

>   Hazardous wastes
>   Hazardous wastes—Environmental aspects
>   Hazardous wastes—Law and legislation
>   Hazardous wastes—United States

**USE PAMPHLET FILE (ALSO CALLED VERTICAL FILE) UNDER THE HEADINGS**

>   Hazardous wastes
>   Pollution

**REFERENCE MATERIALS THAT MAY HELP (BOOKS OR CD-ROMS)**

>   *Editorials on File*. Facts on File.
>   *Facts on File*
>   Magill, Frank N., ed. *Magill's Survey of Science: Earth Science Series*, 1990.
>   *McGraw-Hill Encyclopedia of Science and Technology*, 1992.
>   *The New Book of Popular Science*. Grolier, 1994.
>   General encyclopedias

**PERIODICAL INDEXES TO SEARCH (BOOKS OR CD-ROMS)**

>   EBSCO Magazine Article Summaries
>   InfoTrac
>   NewsBank and other newspaper indexes
>   Readers' Guide to Periodical Literature
>   SIRS (Social Issues Resource Series)
>   WILSONDISC

**ONLINE DATABASES TO SEARCH**

>   America Online
>   CompuServe
>   Dialog

Internet

Prodigy

## KEY WORDS AND DESCRIPTORS FOR PERIODICAL INDEX AND ONLINE SEARCHES

Hazardous wastes

Hazardous waste treatment facilities

Hazardous substances

Hazardous substance disposal

## VIDEOTAPES ON THIS TOPIC

*Cleaning up Toxics at Home*. League of Women Voters, 1990.

*Danger at the Beach*. PBS Video, 1991.

*We All Live Downstream*. Greenpeace USA, 1990.

## FICTION BOOK RELATING TO TOPIC

Sleator, William. *Others See Us*, 1993.

## NATIONAL ORGANIZATIONS TO CONTACT FOR ADDITIONAL INFORMATION

Center for Hazardous Materials Research, 320 William Pitt Way, University of Pittsburgh, Applied Research Center, Pittsburgh, PA 15238.

Citizens Clearinghouse for Hazardous Wastes, P.O. Box 6806, Falls Church, VA 22040.

## SUGGESTIONS FOR NARROWING THIS TOPIC

Choose a specific hazardous material to research; e.g., asbestos, mercury, lead, dioxin.

Create an inventory of household hazardous wastes.

Investigate hazardous waste management.

Write about radioactive waste storage sites.

## SUGGESTIONS FOR RELATED TOPICS

Electromagnetic fields

Carcinogens

Chernobyl

Nuclear arms

Pollution

Recycling

This RESEARCH TOPIC GUIDE is intended to help the library user find information and materials on a particular topic in many sources throughout the library. Resources on this topic are not limited to those described and availability will depend upon the individual library. Feel free to ask a librarian for assistance.

# The Internet

## BACKGROUND

Originally developed by the government as an electronic means of sharing research information, the Internet has mushroomed into a vast network of computer systems and data banks located throughout the world. Information is retrieved and shared in multiple formats by individuals and groups with the equipment necessary to access it.

## BROWSE FOR BOOKS ON THE SHELF USING THESE CALL NUMBERS

    384.3–384.5
    001.64
    004.01
    004.67
    025.04

## LOOK UNDER THE FOLLOWING SUBJECTS IN THE CATALOG (CARD OR COMPUTER)

    Internet (Computer network)
    Computer networks
    Information technology

## REFERENCE MATERIALS THAT MAY HELP (BOOKS OR CD-ROMS)

    Hahn, Harley, and Rick Stout. *The Internet Yellow Pages*, 1995.
    *The New Book of Popular Science*. Grolier, 1994.
    Tennant, Roy, et al. *Crossing the Internet Threshold: An Instructional Handbook*, 1994.
    Zakalik, Joanna. *Gale Guide to Internet Databases*, 1995.
    General encyclopedias

## PERIODICAL INDEXES TO SEARCH (BOOKS OR CD-ROMS)

    EBSCO Magazine Article Summaries
    InfoTrac
    NewsBank and other newspaper indexes
    Readers' Guide to Periodical Literature
    SIRS (Social Issues Resources Series)
    WILSONDISC

## ONLINE DATABASES TO SEARCH

    America Online

CompuServe
Dialog
Internet
Prodigy

## KEY WORDS AND DESCRIPTORS FOR PERIODICAL INDEX AND ONLINE SEARCHES

Internet
Computer networks
Information Superhighway

## VIDEOTAPES ON THIS TOPIC

*Information Superhighway: Understanding and Using the Internet, a Step-by-Step Guide*. Free Range Media, 1994.
*The Internet Show*. Turner Home Entertainment, 1995.

## NATIONAL ORGANIZATION TO CONTACT FOR ADDITIONAL INFORMATION

American Library Association, 50 E. Huron St., Chicago, IL 60611.

## SUGGESTIONS FOR NARROWING THIS TOPIC

Research the history of the Internet.
Discuss ethical issues pertaining to the Internet; e.g., privacy, pornography, free speech.
Investigate the increasing use of e-mail on college campuses.
Describe terminology and slang used on the Internet.
What is the World Wide Web and how is it used?

## SUGGESTIONS FOR RELATED TOPICS

Bill Gates and Microsoft
CD-ROM technology
Computer crime
Interactive video systems
Virtual reality

This RESEARCH TOPIC GUIDE is intended to help the library user find information and materials on a particular topic in many sources throughout the library. Resources on this topic are not limited to those described and availability will depend upon the individual library. Feel free to ask a librarian for assistance.

# Mysterious Circles and Other Ancient Curiosities

## BACKGROUND

Stone circles and carvings, earthen effigies, crop circles, pictographs, and strange engravings have been discovered all over the world. These monuments to early civilizations, still shrouded in mystery and folklore, fascinate researchers and students of history.

## BROWSE FOR BOOKS ON THE SHELF USING THESE CALL NUMBERS

001.94
930–930.12
936.2
942

## LOOK UNDER THE FOLLOWING SUBJECTS IN THE CATALOG (CARD OR COMPUTER)

Megalithic monuments
Megalithic monuments—England—Wiltshire
Stone circles—Great Britain
Stonehenge (England)
Curiosities and wonders

## REFERENCE MATERIALS THAT MAY HELP (BOOKS OR CD-ROMS)

*Mysteries of Mind, Space and Time: The Unexplained*. H.S. Stuttman, 1992.
General encyclopedias

## PERIODICAL INDEXES TO SEARCH (BOOKS OR CD-ROMS)

EBSCO Magazine Article Summaries
InfoTrac
Readers' Guide to Periodical Literature

## ONLINE DATABASES TO SEARCH

America Online
CompuServe
Dialog
Internet

Prodigy

## KEY WORDS AND DESCRIPTORS FOR PERIODICAL INDEX AND ONLINE SEARCHES

Megalithic monuments
Curiosities and wonders
Stonehenge
Crop circles
Ancient astronomy

## VIDEOTAPES ON THIS TOPIC

*Riddle of the Stones*. Pacific Arts Video, 1989.
*Secrets of the Unknown: Stonehenge*. MPI Home Video, 1989.
*Wonders, Sacred and Mysterious*. Reader's Digest, 1994.

## NATIONAL ORGANIZATION TO CONTACT FOR ADDITIONAL INFORMATION

Stonehenge Study Group, 2261 Las Positas Rd., Santa Barbara, CA 93105–4116.

## SUGGESTIONS FOR NARROWING THIS TOPIC

Are crop circles a hoax?
Choose a particular structure to study; e.g., Stonehenge, Avebury, Carnac.
Discuss the connection between Stonehenge and ancient astronomy.

## SUGGESTIONS FOR RELATED TOPICS

Archeology
Celtic myths and legends
Druids
Easter Island statues
Radio carbon dating

This RESEARCH TOPIC GUIDE is intended to help the library user find information and materials on a particular topic in many sources throughout the library. Resources on this topic are not limited to those described and availability will depend upon the individual library. Feel free to ask a librarian for assistance.

# Oceanography

## BACKGROUND

The science that involves all aspects of the ocean, oceanography includes the scientific study of marine life, seawater, ocean floor, waves, tides, and currents. Oceanographers also investigate the oceans' vast resources and their potential use to man.

## BROWSE FOR BOOKS ON THE SHELF USING THESE CALL NUMBERS

551.46
574.92

## LOOK UNDER THE FOLLOWING SUBJECTS IN THE CATALOG (CARD OR COMPUTER)

Oceanography
Marine biology

## USE PAMPHLET FILE (ALSO CALLED VERTICAL FILE) UNDER THE HEADINGS

Oceanography
Ocean
Marine biology

## REFERENCE MATERIALS THAT MAY HELP (BOOKS OR CD-ROMS)

Groves, Donald G., and Lee M. Hunt. *The Ocean World Encyclopedia*, 1980.
Magill, Frank N., ed. *Magill's Survey of Science: Earth Science Series*, 1990.
*McGraw-Hill Encyclopedia of Technology*, 1992.
*The New Book of Popular Science*. Grolier, 1994.
General encyclopedias

## PERIODICAL INDEXES TO SEARCH (BOOKS OR CD-ROMS)

EBSCO Magazine Article Summaries
InfoTrac
NewsBank and other newspaper indexes
Readers' Guide to Periodical Literature
SIRS (Social Issues Resources Series)
WILSONDISC

## ONLINE DATABASES TO SEARCH

America Online
CompuServe

Dialog
Internet
Prodigy

## KEY WORDS AND DESCRIPTORS FOR PERIODICAL INDEX AND ONLINE SEARCHES

Oceanography
Marine biology
Underwater exploration
Ocean bottom
Seawater
Coasts
Marine resources

## VIDEOTAPE ON THIS TOPIC

*Ocean Life*. Transatlantic Video, 1992.

## FICTION BOOKS RELATING TO TOPIC

Norton, Andre. *Sea Siege*, 1980.
Pohl, Frederik, and Jack Williamson. *Land's End*, 1994.
Slonczewski, Joan. *A Door into Ocean*, 1986.

## NATIONAL ORGANIZATIONS TO CONTACT FOR ADDITIONAL INFORMATION

International Oceanographic Foundation, 4600 Rickenbacker Causeway, P.O. Box 499900, Miami, FL 33149–9900.
Oceanic Society, 218 D St., S.E., Washington, DC 20003.

## SUGGESTIONS FOR NARROWING THIS TOPIC

Choose a specific oceanographer to research; e.g., Jacques Cousteau or Robert Ballard.
Discuss the use of robots (or other special equipment) in oceanography.
Investigate hydrothermal vents.
Relate the discovery and exploration of the Titanic.

## SUGGESTIONS FOR RELATED TOPICS

Coral reefs
International law pertaining to oceans
Marine pollution
Ocean as a source of food, oil, minerals, energy, etc.
Submarine geology

This RESEARCH TOPIC GUIDE is intended to help the library user find information and materials on a particular topic in many sources throughout the library. Resources on this topic are not limited to those described and availability will depend upon the individual library. Feel free to ask a librarian for assistance.

# Ozone Depletion

**BACKGROUND**

Many scientists believe the ozone layer in the earth's stratosphere is being depleted due to the use (and release into the atmosphere) of man-made chemicals. The resulting "holes" in the ozone layer allow dangerous levels of ultraviolet radiation to penetrate to the earth's surface. The degree of severity and the solutions to this situation remain topics of debate.

**BROWSE FOR BOOKS ON THE SHELF USING THESE CALL NUMBERS**

> 363.3
> 363.7–363.7392

**LOOK UNDER THE FOLLOWING SUBJECTS IN THE CATALOG (CARD OR COMPUTER)**

> Ozone layer
> Ozone layer depletion
> Chlorofluorocarbons—Environmental aspects

**USE PAMPHLET FILE (ALSO CALLED VERTICAL FILE) UNDER THE HEADINGS**

> Ozone
> Air pollution

**REFERENCE MATERIALS THAT MAY HELP (BOOKS OR CD-ROMS)**

> *CQ Researcher*, April 3, 1992.
> *McGraw-Hill Encyclopedia of Science and Technology*, 1992.
> *The 1994 Information Please Environmental Atlas.* World Resources Institute, 1994.
> *1994 Earth Journal: Environmental Almanac and Resource Directory*, Buzzworm Books, 1994.
> *Today's Science on File.* Facts on File.
> General encyclopedias

**PERIODICAL INDEXES TO SEARCH (BOOKS OR CD-ROMS)**

> EBSCO Magazine Article Summaries
> InfoTrac
> NewsBank and other newspaper indexes
> Readers' Guide to Periodical Literature
> SIRS (Social Issues Resources Series)
> WILSONDISC

**ONLINE DATABASES TO SEARCH**

> America Online
> CompuServe
> Dialog

Internet
Prodigy

## KEY WORDS AND DESCRIPTORS FOR PERIODICAL INDEX AND ONLINE SEARCHES

Ozone
Atmospheric ozone
Ozone layer depletion
Ozonization
Air pollution

## VIDEOTAPES ON THIS TOPIC

*Chemistry: Ozone Blanket in the Air.* Allegro Productions, 1991.
*Hole in the Sky: The Ozone Layer.* Films for the Humanities and Sciences, 1993.
*Spaceship Earth: Our Global Environment.* The Video Project, 1991.

## NATIONAL ORGANIZATIONS TO CONTACT FOR ADDITIONAL INFORMATION

Environmental Defense Fund, 257 Park Ave., S., New York, NY 10010.
Environmental Protection Agency, 401 M St., S.W., Washington, DC 20460.
World Resources Institute, 1709 New York Ave., N.W., Ste. 700, Washington, DC 20006.

## SUGGESTIONS FOR NARROWING THIS TOPIC

Investigate the possible effects of ozone depletion on the ocean.
How do the eruptions of volcanoes effect ozone depletion?
Research ozone–depleting chemicals such as chlorofluorocarbons and halons.
Are warnings about ozone depletion exaggerated? Discuss.
Comment on the possible connection between ozone depletion and skin cancer.

## SUGGESTIONS FOR RELATED TOPICS

Acid rain
Air pollution
Greenhouse effect
Ozone as a pollutant
Volcanoes

This RESEARCH TOPIC GUIDE is intended to help the library user find information and materials on a particular topic in many sources throughout the library. Resources on this topic are not limited to those described and availability will depend upon the individual library. Feel free to ask a librarian for assistance.

# Quarks

**BACKGROUND**

The fundamental units of matter, quarks come in six "flavors," each with several "colors." In combination, quarks form protons, neutrons, and mesons. The recent discovery of the "top quark" brought great excitement to the world of nuclear physics.

**BROWSE FOR BOOKS ON THE SHELF USING THESE CALL NUMBERS**

> 539
> 539.7–539.721
> 530.12–530.142

**LOOK UNDER THE FOLLOWING SUBJECTS IN THE CATALOG (CARD OR COMPUTER)**

> Quarks
> Particles (Nuclear physics)

**USE PAMPHLET FILE (ALSO CALLED VERTICAL FILE) UNDER THE HEADING**

> Physics

**REFERENCE MATERIALS THAT MAY HELP (BOOKS OR CD-ROMS)**

> Asimov, Isaac. *Asimov's Chronology of Science and Discovery*, 1994.
> Hetherington, Norriss, ed. *Encyclopedia of Cosmology: Historical, Philosophical, and Scientific Foundations of Modern Cosmology*, 1993.
> Magill, Frank N., ed. *Great Events from History II: Science and Technology Series*, 1991.
> *McGraw-Hill Encyclopedia of Science and Technology*, 1992.
> *Today's Science on File*. Facts on File.
> General encyclopedias

**PERIODICAL INDEXES TO SEARCH (BOOKS OR CD-ROMS)**

> EBSCO Magazine Article Summaries
> InfoTrac
> NewsBank and other newspaper indexes
> Readers' Guide to Periodical Literature
> SIRS (Social Issues Resources Series)
> WILSONDISC

## ONLINE DATABASES TO SEARCH

America Online
CompuServe
Dialog
Internet
Prodigy

## KEY WORDS AND DESCRIPTORS FOR PERIODICAL INDEX AND ONLINE SEARCHES

Quarks
Gluons
Particles (Nuclear physics)
Quantum flavor dynamics

## VIDEOTAPES ON THIS TOPIC

*A Brief History of Time*. Paramount Home Video, 1992.
*Creation of the Universe*. Northstar Productions, 1985.

## SUGGESTIONS FOR NARROWING THIS TOPIC

Discuss the scientific equipment used in quark research.
Explain the attributes of quarks; e.g., behavior.
Investigate the quark family of subatomic particles; e.g., "flavors" and "colors."
Relate the discovery of quarks.
Research the discovery of the "top quark."

## SUGGESTIONS FOR RELATED TOPICS

Enrico Fermi
Big Bang theory
Black holes
Nuclear physics
Quantum theory
Stephen Hawking

This RESEARCH TOPIC GUIDE is intended to help the library user find information and materials on a particular topic in many sources throughout the library. Resources on this topic are not limited to those described and availability will depend upon the individual library. Feel free to ask a librarian for assistance.

# Rain Forest Destruction

## BACKGROUND

The rain forests of the world are disappearing at an alarming rate. Demands for timber, forest products, and development are but a few of the many causes of forest destruction. This massive loss of trees affects our environment in devastating ways, causing flooding, desertification, famine, extinction of rain forest plants and animals, and may even hasten the global warming process.

## BROWSE FOR BOOKS ON THE SHELF USING THESE CALL NUMBERS

574.5–574.52642
574.72
333.7516

## LOOK UNDER THE FOLLOWING SUBJECTS IN THE CATALOG (CARD OR COMPUTER)

Rain forest ecology
Rain forests (Rain forests—Brazil, Rain forests—Mexico, etc.)
Rain forest conservation
Deforestation

## USE PAMPHLET FILE (ALSO CALLED VERTICAL FILE) UNDER THE HEADINGS

Rain forests

## REFERENCE MATERIALS THAT MAY HELP (BOOKS OR CD-ROMS)

*CQ Researcher*, September 20, 1991.
*The International Book of the Forests*. Simon & Schuster, 1981.
*McGraw-Hill Encyclopedia of Science and Technology*, 1992.
*The New Book of Popular Science*. Grolier, 1994.

## PERIODICAL INDEXES TO SEARCH (BOOKS OR CD-ROMS)

EBSCO Magazine Article Summaries
InfoTrac
NewsBank and other newspaper indexes
Readers' Guide to Periodical Literature
SIRS (Social Issues Resources Series)
WILSONDISC

## ONLINE DATABASES TO SEARCH

America Online
CompuServe
Dialog
Internet
Prodigy

## KEY WORDS AND DESCRIPTORS FOR PERIODICAL INDEX AND ONLINE SEARCHES

Rain forests (also try rainforests)
Rain forest ecology
Rain forest plants
Rain forest fauna
Deforestation

## VIDEOTAPES ON THIS TOPIC

*Tropical Rainforest*. Finley-Holiday Films, 1992.
*You Can't Grow Home Again*. Children's Television Workshop, 1990.

## NATIONAL ORGANIZATIONS TO CONTACT FOR ADDITIONAL INFORMATION

Rain Forest Action Network, 450 Sansome St., Ste. 700, San Francisco, CA 94111.
Rain Forest Alliance, 270 Lafayette St., Ste. 512, New York, NY 10012.
World Wildlife Fund, 1250 24th St., N.W., Washington, DC 20037.

## SUGGESTIONS FOR NARROWING THIS TOPIC

Analyze a specific rain forest or country; e.g., Belize, Mexico.
Discuss rain forest wildlife and the loss of habitat.
Research the indigenous people of the rain forest.
Research products from the rain forest.

## SUGGESTIONS FOR RELATED TOPICS

Clearcutting
Deforestation
Desertification
Timber industry

This RESEARCH TOPIC GUIDE is intended to help the library user find information and materials on a particular topic in many sources throughout the library. Resources on this topic are not limited to those described and availability will depend upon the individual library. Feel free to ask a librarian for assistance.

# Unidentified Flying Objects (UFOs)

**BACKGROUND**

Since June 1947, when a pilot reported seeing a silvery saucer-shaped ball speeding over the Cascade Mountains of Washington State, UFOs, or flying saucers, have been a hotly debated topic. Alleged encounters have run the gamut from friendly to hostile, including abductions. Although the U.S. government and the majority of the scientific community believe there is no solid evidence of the existence of UFOs, many others are convinced of their reality.

**BROWSE FOR BOOKS ON THE SHELF USING THESE CALL NUMBERS**

> 001.9
> 001.74
> 133.03

**LOOK UNDER THE FOLLOWING SUBJECTS IN THE CATALOG (CARD OR COMPUTER)**

> Unidentified flying objects
> Flying saucers

**USE PAMPHLET FILE (ALSO CALLED VERTICAL FILE) UNDER THE HEADINGS**

> Unidentified flying objects
> UFOs

**REFERENCE MATERIALS THAT MAY HELP (BOOKS OR CD-ROMS)**

> Makower, Joel, and Marilyn Fenichel, eds. *The Air and Space Catalog: The Complete Source Book to Everything in the Universe*, 1989.
> *Mysteries of Mind, Space and Time: The Unexplained.* H. S. Stuttman, 1992.
> *The New Book of Popular Science.* Grolier, 1994.

**PERIODICAL INDEXES TO SEARCH (BOOKS OR CD-ROMS)**

> EBSCO Magazine Article Summaries
> InfoTrac
> NewsBank and other newspaper indexes
> Readers' Guide to Periodical Literature
> SIRS (Social Issues Resources Series)
> WILSONDISC

**ONLINE DATABASES TO SEARCH**

> America Online
> CompuServe

Dialog
Internet
Prodigy

## KEY WORDS AND DESCRIPTORS FOR PERIODICAL INDEX AND ONLINE SEARCHES

Unidentified flying objects
UFOs
Flying saucers
Extraterrestrial beings
Roswell incident

## VIDEOTAPES ON THIS TOPIC

*Close Encounters of the Third Kind*. Columbia Pictures Home Entertainment, 1980.
*UFOs: Are We Alone?* Vestron Video, 1988.
*UFOs: The Unsolved Mystery*. Seligman Productions, 1989.

## FICTION BOOKS RELATING TO TOPIC

Chetwin, Grace. *Collidescope*, 1990.
Goodwin, Godfrey. *The Janissaries*, 1943. (adult)
Spielberg, Steven. *Close Encounters of the Third Kind*, 1977.

## NATIONAL ORGANIZATIONS TO CONTACT FOR ADDITIONAL INFORMATION

Fair-Witness Project, 4219 W. Olive St., Burbank, CA 91505.
Fund for UFO Research, P.O. Box 277, Mt. Rainier, MD 20712.

## SUGGESTIONS FOR NARROWING THIS TOPIC

Analyze reported encounters for consistencies.
Discuss possible governmental coverups.
Investigate current research into UFOs.
Report on one or more specific cases of alleged encounters; e.g., Roswell, NM, in 1947 or Hillsdale, MI, in 1966.

## SUGGESTIONS FOR RELATED TOPICS

False memory syndrome
Life on other planets
Unidentified submarine objects

This RESEARCH TOPIC GUIDE is intended to help the library user find information and materials on a particular topic in many sources throughout the library. Resources on this topic are not limited to those described and availability will depend upon the individual library. Feel free to ask a librarian for assistance.

# Virtual Reality

**BACKGROUND**

The technology of virtual reality (electronic sensors and computer-generated images) creates new ultrarealistic worlds for people to explore. Seated at computers, in theaters, and at game arcades, wearing data gloves, headsets, or visors, participants can experience cyberspace. Virtual reality is used to train doctors, astronauts, and pilots to perform complex procedures; it is also used to provide recreational outlets. However, controversial and ethical questions over the use of virtual reality have emerged.

**BROWSE FOR BOOKS ON THE SHELF USING THESE CALL NUMBERS**

>006–006.1
>501.3

**LOOK UNDER THE FOLLOWING SUBJECTS IN THE CATALOG (CARD OR COMPUTER)**

>Virtual reality
>Cybernetics
>Human-computer interaction

**REFERENCE MATERIALS THAT MAY HELP (BOOKS OR CD-ROMS)**

>*McGraw-Hill Yearbook of Science and Technology*, 1992.
>*The New Book of Popular Science*. Grolier, 1994.
>General encyclopedias

**PERIODICAL INDEXES TO SEARCH (BOOKS OR CD-ROMS)**

>EBSCO Magazine Article Summaries
>InfoTrac
>NewsBank and other newspaper indexes
>Readers' Guide to Periodical Literature
>SIRS (Social Issues Resources Series)
>WILSONDISC

**ONLINE DATABASES TO SEARCH**

>America Online
>CompuServe
>Dialog
>Internet
>Prodigy

**KEY WORDS AND DESCRIPTORS FOR PERIODICAL INDEX AND ONLINE SEARCHES**

Virtual reality

**VIDEOTAPES ON THIS TOPIC**

*Virtual Reality*. Media Magic, 1990.
*Wild Palms*. ABC Video, 1993.

**FICTION BOOKS RELATING TO TOPIC**

Cross, Gillian. *New World*, 1995.
Hawke, Simon. *The Whims of Creation*, 1995.
Scott, Michael. *Gemini*, 1994.

**NATIONAL ORGANIZATIONS TO CONTACT FOR ADDITIONAL INFORMATION**

Computer Professionals for Social Responsibility, P.O. Box 717, Palo Alto, CA 94301.
Virtual Environment/Teleoperator Research Consortium, Massachusetts Institute of Technology, 77 Massachusetts Ave., Cambridge, MA 02139.

**SUGGESTIONS FOR NARROWING THIS TOPIC**

Comment on the use of virtual reality in the courtroom.
Discuss the moral and ethical aspects of using virtual reality technology.
Investigate the uses of virtual reality in industry, the military, the space program, or education.
Research virtual reality games; e.g., Doom, Dactyl Nightmare.

**SUGGESTIONS FOR RELATED TOPICS**

Computer graphics
Holograms
Interactive computer systems; e.g., interactive books

This RESEARCH TOPIC GUIDE is intended to help the library user find information and materials on a particular topic in many sources throughout the library. Resources on this topic are not limited to those described and availability will depend upon the individual library. Feel free to ask a librarian for assistance.

# Volcanoes

**BACKGROUND**

Volcanoes are steep hills or mountains formed by an accumulation of molten rock forced through openings in the earth's crust. These volcanic vents, or openings, are referred to as volcanoes when actively spewing magma (molten rock).

**BROWSE FOR BOOKS ON THE SHELF USING THESE CALL NUMBERS**

> 551.59
> 551.2

**LOOK UNDER THE FOLLOWING SUBJECTS IN THE CATALOG (CARD OR COMPUTER)**

> Volcanoes
> Volcanoes—Hawaii
> Volcanoes—United States

**USE PAMPHLET FILE (ALSO CALLED VERTICAL FILE) UNDER THE HEADING**

> Volcanoes

**REFERENCE MATERIALS THAT MAY HELP (BOOKS OR CD-ROMS)**

> *Editorial Research Reports*, October 21, 1983.
> Magill, Frank N., ed. *Magill's Survey of Science: Earth Science Series*, 1990.
> *McGraw-Hill Encyclopedia of Science and Technology*, 1992.
> *The New Book of Popular Science*. Grolier, 1994.
> Ritchie, David. *The Encyclopedia of Earthquakes and Volcanoes*, 1994.
> Simkin, Tom, and Lee Siebert. *Volcanoes of the World*, 1994.
> General encyclopedias

**PERIODICAL INDEXES TO SEARCH (BOOKS OR CD-ROMS)**

> EBSCO Magazine Article Summaries
> InfoTrac
> NewsBank and other newspaper indexes
> SIRS (Social Issues Resources Series)
> WILSONDISC

**ONLINE DATABASES TO SEARCH**

> America Online
> CompuServe
> Dialog

Internet
Prodigy

## KEY WORDS AND DESCRIPTORS FOR PERIODICAL INDEX AND ONLINE SEARCHES

Volcanoes
Volcanic activity prediction
Mt. St. Helens
Volcanic ash

## VIDEOTAPES ON THIS TOPIC

*Story of America's Great Volcanoes*. Questar, 1992.
*Volcanoscapes: Peles March to the Pacific*. Tropical Visions Video, 1987.

## FICTION BOOKS RELATING TO TOPIC

Campbell, Eric. *The Shark Callers*, 1994.
Kendall, Carol. *The Tirelings*, 1982.
Moran, Richard. *The Empire of Ice*, 1994.

## NATIONAL ORGANIZATION TO CONTACT FOR ADDITIONAL INFORMATION

Inter-Association Commission on Tsunami, C/O Pacific Marine Environmental Laboratory, 7600 Sand Point Way, N.E., Bldg. 3, Seattle, WA
98115–0070.

## SUGGESTIONS FOR NARROWING THIS TOPIC

Analyze the recreational aspects of volcanoes.
Discuss the environmental aspects of volcanic eruptions.
Choose a specific volcano to report on; e.g., Haleakala, Kilauea, Mt. St.
Helens.
Investigate volcanoes in history; e.g., Mt. Vesuvius or Mt. Etna.
Research volcanic activity on Mars.

## SUGGESTIONS FOR RELATED TOPICS

Earthquakes
Plate Tectonics
Tsunamis (tidal waves)

This RESEARCH TOPIC GUIDE is intended to help the library user find information and
materials on a particular topic in many sources throughout the library. Resources on this
topic are not limited to those described and availability will depend upon the individual
library. Feel free to ask a librarian for assistance.

# II

# Social Issues Research
# Topic Guides

# Abortion

## BACKGROUND

Of the many controversies facing America in the 1990s, the abortion issue seems the most divisive and damaging. As pro-choice and pro-life forces battle in the press and at the picket lines, women are left wondering about their options and legal rights.

## BROWSE FOR BOOKS ON THE SHELF USING THESE CALL NUMBERS

363.46–363.4609
613.943
618.88

## LOOK UNDER THE FOLLOWING SUBJECTS IN THE CATALOG (CARD OR COMPUTER)

Abortion

Try one of the many subject headings beginning with Abortion; e.g., Abortion—Moral and ethical aspects.

## USE PAMPHLET FILE (ALSO CALLED VERTICAL FILE) UNDER THE HEADING

Abortion

## REFERENCE MATERIALS THAT MAY HELP (BOOKS OR CD-ROMS)

*CQ Researcher*, July 5, 1991; April 8, 1994; April 7, 1995.
Harrison, Maureen, and Steve Gilbert, eds. *Abortion Decisions of the United States*. (series)
Hempelman, Kathleen. *Teen Legal Rights: A Guide for the '90s*, 1994.
Shapiro, Ian. *Abortion: The Supreme Court Decisions*, 1995.

## PERIODICAL INDEXES TO SEARCH (BOOKS OR CD-ROMS)

EBSCO Magazine Article Summaries
InfoTrac
NewsBank and other newspaper indexes
Readers' Guide to Periodical Literature
SIRS (Social Issues Resources Series)
WILSONDISC

## ONLINE DATABASES TO SEARCH

America Online
CompuServe
Dialog
Internet
Prodigy

## KEY WORDS AND DESCRIPTORS FOR PERIODICAL INDEX AND ONLINE SEARCHES

Abortion
Teenage abortion
Pro-choice
Pro-life
*Roe vs. Wade*

## VIDEOTAPES ON THIS TOPIC

*Abortion: Desperate Choices*. Ambrose Video, 1992.
*Roe vs. Wade*. Paramount Home Video, 1989.
*What's the Common Ground on Abortion?* Common Ground–WNYC Productions, 1989.

## FICTION BOOKS RELATING TO TOPIC

Irving, John. *The Cider House Rules*, 1985. (adult)
Klein, Norma. *Beginners' Love*, 1983.
Kurland, Morton L. *Our Sacred Honor*, 1986.
Zindel, Paul. *My Darling, My Hamburger*, 1969.

## NATIONAL ORGANIZATIONS TO CONTACT FOR ADDITIONAL INFORMATION

American Life Lobby, P.O. Box 1350, Stafford, VA 22555.
National Abortion Rights Action League, 1156 15th St., N.W., Ste. 700, Washington, DC 20005.
Planned Parenthood Federation of America, 810 7th Ave., New York, NY 10019.

## SUGGESTIONS FOR NARROWING THIS TOPIC

Discuss the moral and ethical aspects of abortion.
Investigate the law and legislation regarding abortion.
Research abortion and the Supreme Court.
Report on the medical, psychological, or religious aspects of abortion.

## SUGGESTIONS FOR RELATED TOPICS

Abortion clinics
Adoption
Birth control
Fetal tissue research
Pro-choice movement
Pro-life movement

This RESEARCH TOPIC GUIDE is intended to help the library user find information and materials on a particular topic in many sources throughout the library. Resources on this topic are not limited to those described and availability will depend upon the individual library. Feel free to ask a librarian for assistance.

# Affirmative Action

**BACKGROUND**

Affirmative action, originally voluntary, is now a legislated system often requiring employers to hire a certain percentage of their workers from minority groups. The intent of the law is to make up for past discrimination while protecting minorities from bias in the workplace. Opponents call affirmative action reverse discrimination in its treatment of white males.

**BROWSE FOR BOOKS ON THE SHELF USING THESE CALL NUMBERS**

> 342.73–342.7308
> 331.133–331.3

**LOOK UNDER THE FOLLOWING SUBJECTS IN THE CATALOG (CARD OR COMPUTER)**

> Affirmative action programs—United States
> Minorities—Employment—United States
> Discrimination in employment—Law and legislation—United States
> Discrimination in employment—United States

**REFERENCE MATERIALS THAT MAY HELP (BOOKS OR CD-ROMS)**

> Berry, Stephen L., et al. *Employment Law Handbook: A Complete Reference for Business*, 1993.
> *CQ Researcher*, April 28, 1995.
> Magill, Frank N., ed. *Great Events from History II: Human Rights Series*, 1992.
> Patrick, John J. *The Young Oxford Companion to the Supreme Court of the United States*, 1994.

**PERIODICAL INDEXES TO SEARCH (BOOKS OR CD-ROMS)**

> EBSCO Magazine Article Summaries
> InfoTrac
> NewsBank and other newspaper indexes
> Readers' Guide to Periodical Literature
> SIRS (Social Issues Resources Series)
> WILSONDISC

**ONLINE DATABASES TO SEARCH**

> America Online
> CompuServe
> Dialog

Internet
Prodigy

## KEY WORDS AND DESCRIPTORS FOR PERIODICAL INDEX AND ONLINE SEARCHES

Affirmative action
Affirmative action programs
Minorities—employment
Blacks—employment
Racial quotas
Reverse discrimination in employment
Equal Employment Opportunities Commission (EEOC)
Minority business
Discrimination in employment

## VIDEOTAPE ON THIS TOPIC

*The Constitution: That Delicate Balance*, Vol. 12. Films, Inc., 1984.

## NATIONAL ORGANIZATIONS TO CONTACT FOR ADDITIONAL INFORMATION

American Association for Affirmative Action, 11 E. Hubbard St., Ste. 200, Chicago, IL 60611.

Institute for Justice, 1001 Pennsylvania Ave., N.W., Washington, DC 20004.

NAACP Legal Defense and Education Fund, 1275 K St., N.W., Ste. 301, Washington, DC 20006.

## SUGGESTIONS FOR NARROWING THIS TOPIC

Analyze the constitutionality of affirmative action programs.
Discuss the impact of affirmative action on the college admissions process.
Discuss the moral and ethical aspects of affirmative action.
Investigate the status of federally sponsored affirmative action programs.
Present the case for (or against) affirmative action.

## SUGGESTIONS FOR RELATED TOPICS

Alternatives to affirmative action
Civil rights movement
Glass ceiling
Reverse discrimination

This RESEARCH TOPIC GUIDE is intended to help the library user find information and materials on a particular topic in many sources throughout the library. Resources on this topic are not limited to those described and availability will depend upon the individual library. Feel free to ask a librarian for assistance.

# Aging

**BACKGROUND**

Over 30 million Americans are sixty-five years of age or older according to U.S. Census figures. This represents 12.8 percent of the population compared with less than 1 percent in 1900. Reductions in death rates account for the increase in older Americans. The aging of the population introduces many medical, social, and ethical issues into the public debate.

**BROWSE FOR BOOKS ON THE SHELF USING THESE CALL NUMBERS**

> 362.6–362.82
> 305.26–305.2609
> 306.7
> 301.435
> 174.2
> 613.0438
> 649.8

**LOOK UNDER THE FOLLOWING SUBJECTS IN THE CATALOG (CARD OR COMPUTER)**

> Aging
> Aged
> Aged—Health and hygiene
> Geriatrics
> Gerontology
> Old age

**REFERENCE MATERIALS THAT MAY HELP (BOOKS OR CD-ROMS)**

> Beanstalk, Robert H., and Linda K. George, eds. *Handbook of Aging and the Social Sciences*, 1995.
>
> Manheimer, Ronald J., ed. *Older Americans Almanac: A Reference Work on Seniors in the United States*, 1994.
>
> McLerran, Jennifer, and Patrick McKee. *Old Age in Myth and Symbol: A Cultural Dictionary*, 1991.
>
> Roy, F. Hampton, and Charles Russell. *The Encyclopedia of Aging and the Elderly*, 1992.
>
> Schick, Frank L., and Renee Schick, ed. *Statistical Handbook on Aging Americans, 1994*, 1994.

**PERIODICAL INDEXES TO SEARCH (BOOKS OR CD-ROMS)**

> EBSCO Magazine Article Summaries
> InfoTrac
> NewsBank and other newspaper indexes
> Readers' Guide to Periodical Literature

SIRS (Social Issues Resources Series)
WILSONDISC

## ONLINE DATABASES TO SEARCH

America Online
CompuServe
Dialog
Internet
Prodigy

## KEY WORDS AND DESCRIPTORS FOR PERIODICAL INDEX AND ONLINE SEARCHES

Aged
Aging
Elderly
Geriatrics
Gerontology
Old age

## VIDEOTAPES ON THIS TOPIC

*Final Choices*. Retirement Research Foundation, 1987.
*Healthy Aging*. Healthscope Film Library, 1986.
*The Mind: Aging*. PBS Video, 1988.
*On Golden Pond*. CBS/Fox Video, 1981.

## FICTION BOOK RELATING TO TOPIC

Martz, Sandra. *When I Am an Old Woman I Shall Wear Purple*, 1991.

## NATIONAL ORGANIZATION TO CONTACT FOR ADDITIONAL INFORMATION

American Association of Retired Persons (AARP), 601 E St., N.W., Washington, DC 20049.

## SUGGESTIONS FOR NARROWING THIS TOPIC

Discuss the psychological, physiological, or philosophical aspects of aging.
Find out about adult day care centers or nursing homes.
How is medical care for the elderly handled in the United States?
Investigate the treatment of aging in different countries.

## SUGGESTIONS FOR RELATED TOPICS

Assisted suicide
Medical ethics
Mental health services
Pediatrics

This RESEARCH TOPIC GUIDE is intended to help the library user find information and materials on a particular topic in many sources throughout the library. Resources on this topic are not limited to those described and availability will depend upon the individual library. Feel free to ask a librarian for assistance.

# AIDS (Acquired Immunodeficiency Syndrome)

**BACKGROUND**

The AIDS epidemic has existed in the United States for over fifteen years and a solution to the crisis is nowhere in sight. Hope is fading for an AIDS vaccine to be developed in the near future. No longer solely a disease of homosexuals, AIDS infects all populations. Scientists, however, are still determined to focus their efforts on HIV virus research.

**BROWSE FOR BOOKS ON THE SHELF USING THESE CALL NUMBERS**

> 616.9–616.9792
> 362.1969–362.19892

**LOOK UNDER THE FOLLOWING SUBJECTS IN THE CATALOG (CARD OR COMPUTER)**

> AIDS (Disease)
> Try one of the many subject headings beginning AIDS (Disease); e.g., AIDS (Disease)—History.

**USE PAMPHLET FILE (ALSO CALLED VERTICAL FILE) UNDER THE HEADING**

> AIDS

**REFERENCE MATERIALS THAT MAY HELP (BOOKS OR CD-ROMS)**

> *CQ Researcher*, December 25, 1992; April 21, 1995.
> Huber, Jeffrey T., ed. *How to Find Information about AIDS*, 1992.
> Kloser, Patricia, and Jane MacLean Craig. *The Woman's HIV Sourcebook*, 1994.
> World Health Organization. *AIDS: Images of the Epidemic*, 1994.
> General encyclopedias

**PERIODICAL INDEXES TO SEARCH (BOOKS OR CD-ROMS)**

> EBSCO Magazine Article Summaries
> InfoTrac
> NewsBank and other newspaper indexes
> Readers' Guide to Periodical Literature
> SIRS (Social Issues Resources Series)
> WILSONDISC

**ONLINE DATABASES TO SEARCH**

> America Online
> CompuServe
> Dialog

Internet

Prodigy

## KEY WORDS AND DESCRIPTORS FOR PERIODICAL INDEX AND ONLINE SEARCHES

AIDS

HIV virus

AIDS patients

## VIDEOTAPES ON THIS TOPIC

*Common Threads: Stories from the Quilt.* Direct Cinema, 1994.

*And the Band Played On.* HBO Video, 1993.

*Time Out: The Truth about HIV, AIDS, and You.* Paramount, 1992.

## FICTION BOOKS RELATING TO TOPIC

Kerr, M. E. *Night Kites*, 1986.

Miklowitz, Gloria D. *Good-Bye Tomorrow*, 1987.

Nelson, Theresa. *Earthshine*, 1994.

## NATIONAL ORGANIZATIONS TO CONTACT FOR ADDITIONAL INFORMATION

AIDS Action Council, 1875 Connecticut Ave., N.W., Ste. 700, Washington, DC 20009.

American Foundation for AIDS Research, 733 Third Ave., 12th Fl., New York, NY 10017.

CDC National AIDS Clearinghouse, P.O. Box 6003, Rockville, MD 20849–6003.

## SUGGESTIONS FOR NARROWING THIS TOPIC

Examine the social aspects of the AIDS epidemic.

Discuss AIDS prevention.

Discuss treatment for AIDS.

Research AIDS in adolescents and/or children.

What is the AIDS quilt and why is it important?

## SUGGESTIONS FOR RELATED TOPICS

Epidemics in history; e.g., bubonic plague, flu, ebola virus.

AIDS activists

Chlamydia

Famous victims of AIDS; e.g., Ryan White, Magic Johnson, Arthur Ashe

Gay rights

Herpes

This RESEARCH TOPIC GUIDE is intended to help the library user find information and materials on a particular topic in many sources throughout the library. Resources on this topic are not limited to those described and availability will depend upon the individual library. Feel free to ask a librarian for assistance.

# Animal Experimentation

**BACKGROUND**

The results of using animal experimentation for research have provided us with insulin, pacemakers, organ transplants, nutritional supplements, and many other benefits. Animal experimentation is also used in cosmetics and other consumer industries. The debate among scientists, animal rights activists, and consumers over whether or not to experiment on animals has become heated and sometimes violent.

**BROWSE FOR BOOKS ON THE SHELF USING THESE CALL NUMBERS**

>  174.3
>  179.3

**LOOK UNDER THE FOLLOWING SUBJECTS IN THE CATALOG (CARD OR COMPUTER)**

>  Animal rights
>  Animal welfare
>  Animal experimentation
>  Animal experimentation—Moral and ethical aspects
>  Vivisection
>  Animal rights activists

**USE PAMPHLET FILE (ALSO CALLED VERTICAL FILE) UNDER THE HEADINGS**

>  Animal rights
>  Animal welfare

**REFERENCE MATERIALS THAT MAY HELP (BOOKS OR CD-ROMS)**

>  *CQ Researcher*, May 24, 1991.
>  Sherry, Clifford J. *Animal Rights: A Reference Handbook*, 1994.

**PERIODICAL INDEXES TO SEARCH (BOOKS OR CD-ROMS)**

>  EBSCO Magazine Article Summaries
>  InfoTrac
>  NewsBank and other newspaper indexes
>  Readers' Guide to Periodical Literature
>  SIRS (Social Issues Resources Series)
>  WILSONDISC

**ONLINE DATABASES TO SEARCH**

>  America Online
>  CompuServe
>  Dialog
>  Internet
>  Prodigy

# KEY WORDS AND DESCRIPTORS FOR PERIODICAL INDEX AND ONLINE SEARCHES

Animal experimentation
Animal rights
Animal rights groups
Animal rights movement
Animal welfare
Vivisection
Laboratory animals
Medical research—Animal experimentation

## VIDEOTAPES ON THIS TOPIC

*Animal Rights: Here and Now Series*, Heretic, 1990.
*Throwaways*. ASPCA, 1991.

## FICTION BOOKS RELATING TO TOPIC

Keller, Beverly. *Fowl Play, Desdemona*, 1989.
Wells, H. G. *Island of Doctor Moreau*, many editions.

## NATIONAL ORGANIZATIONS TO CONTACT FOR ADDITIONAL INFORMATION

American Anti-Vivisection Society, Noble Plaza, Ste. 204, 801 Old York Rd., Jenkintown, PA 19046.
Foundation for Biomedical Research, 818 Connecticut Ave., N.W., Ste. 303, Washington, DC 20006.

## SUGGESTIONS FOR NARROWING THIS TOPIC

Discuss the moral and ethical aspects of animal experimentation.
Discuss the use of animal experimentation in medical research, agriculture, or consumer products.
Investigate the treatment of laboratory animals.
Report on an animal rights activist group; e.g., Animal Liberation Front.
What are alternatives to animal experimentation?

## SUGGESTIONS FOR RELATED TOPICS

Anti-fur movement
Hunting
Zoos

This RESEARCH TOPIC GUIDE is intended to help the library user find information and materials on a particular topic in many sources throughout the library. Resources on this topic are not limited to those described and availability will depend upon the individual library. Feel free to ask a librarian for assistance.

# Assisted Suicide

**BACKGROUND**

Brought to the headlines by Dr. Jack Kevorkian, assisted suicide should not be confused with euthanasia. In assisted suicide a physician, or other party, provides a terminally ill patient with the means to take his or her own life. In contrast, euthanasia involves the physician's administering the lethal drug. The ethical, moral, and legal aspects of assisted suicide are being debated in the courts, the press, schools, and homes across the country.

**BROWSE FOR BOOKS ON THE SHELF USING THESE CALL NUMBERS**

179.7
362.175

**LOOK UNDER THE FOLLOWING SUBJECTS IN THE CATALOG (CARD OR COMPUTER)**

Assisted suicide
Suicide
Right to die

**USE PAMPHLET FILE (ALSO CALLED VERTICAL FILE) UNDER THE HEADING**

Suicide

**REFERENCE MATERIALS THAT MAY HELP (BOOKS OR CD-ROMS)**

*CQ Researcher*, February 21, 1992; May 5, 1995.
Dunstan, Duncan, et al., eds. *Dictionary of Medical Ethics*, 1981.
Evans, Glen, and Norman L. Farberow. *The Encyclopedia of Suicide*, 1988.
Kastenbaum, Robert, and Beatrice Kastenbaum, eds. *Encyclopedia of Death*, 1993.

**PERIODICAL INDEXES TO SEARCH (BOOKS OR CD-ROMS)**

EBSCO Magazine Article Summaries
InfoTrac
NewsBank and other newspaper indexes
Readers' Guide to Periodical Literature
SIRS (Social Issues Resources Series)
WILSONDISC

**ONLINE DATABASES TO SEARCH**

America Online
CompuServe

Dialog
Internet
Prodigy

## KEY WORDS AND DESCRIPTORS FOR PERIODICAL INDEX AND ONLINE SEARCHES

Assisted suicide
Euthanasia
Kevorkian, Jack
Right to die
Right to life
Right to refuse treatment
Suicide

## VIDEOTAPE ON THIS TOPIC

*What's the Common Ground on Euthanasia?* Common Ground–WNYC Productions, 1989.

## NATIONAL ORGANIZATIONS TO CONTACT FOR ADDITIONAL INFORMATION

Center for the Rights of the Terminally Ill, P.O. Box 54246, Hurst, TX 76054–2064.
Choice in Dying—The National Council for the Right to Die, 200 Varick St., New York, NY 10014.
Hemlock Society, P.O. Box 11830, Eugene, OR 97440–4030.
International Anti-Euthanasia Task Force, University of Steubenville Human Life Center, Steubenville, OH 43952.

## SUGGESTIONS FOR NARROWING THIS TOPIC

Discuss Dr. Jack Kevorkian's role in bringing assisted suicide to public attention.
Discuss the use of assisted suicide among AIDS patients.
Investigate the legal aspects of assisted suicide.
Research the clinical criteria for physician-assisted suicide.

## SUGGESTIONS FOR RELATED TOPICS

Living wills
Hospice movement
Rights of the terminally ill
Suicide prevention among teens

This RESEARCH TOPIC GUIDE is intended to help the library user find information and materials on a particular topic in many sources throughout the library. Resources on this topic are not limited to those described and availability will depend upon the individual library. Feel free to ask a librarian for assistance.

# Capital Punishment

## BACKGROUND

Legal in a majority of states, capital punishment continues to be fiercely debated. At issue are its effects on criminals, victims, the justice system, and society as a whole. Does the threat of capital punishment deter crime? Can we justify the fact that sometimes innocent people are put to death?

## BROWSE FOR BOOKS ON THE SHELF USING THESE CALL NUMBERS

364.66–364.73
174.24

## LOOK UNDER THE FOLLOWING SUBJECTS IN THE CATALOG (CARD OR COMPUTER)

Capital punishment
Capital punishment—United States

## USE PAMPHLET FILE (ALSO CALLED VERTICAL FILE) UNDER THE HEADING

Capital punishment

## REFERENCE MATERIALS THAT MAY HELP (BOOKS OR CD-ROMS)

*CQ Researcher*, March 10, 1995.
*Editorial Research Reports*, July 13, 1990.
Kastenbaum, Robert, and Beatrice Kastenbaum, eds. *Encyclopedia of Death*, 1993.
Kronenwetter, Michael. *Capital Punishment: A Reference Handbook*, 1993.
Patrick, John J. *The Young Oxford Companion to the Supreme Court of the United States*, 1994.
General encyclopedias

## PERIODICAL INDEXES TO SEARCH (BOOKS OR CD-ROMS)

EBSCO Magazine Article Summaries
InfoTrac
NewsBank and other newspaper indexes
Readers' Guide to Periodical Literature
SIRS (Social Issues Resources Series)
WILSONDISC

## ONLINE DATABASES TO SEARCH

America Online
CompuServe
Dialog
Internet
Prodigy

## KEY WORDS AND DESCRIPTORS FOR PERIODICAL INDEX AND ONLINE SEARCHES

Capital punishment
Death penalty
Death row
Executions
Executions and executioners
Hanging
Electric chair

## VIDEOTAPES ON THIS TOPIC

*Death Penalty*. Films for the Humanities and Sciences, 1988.
*The Next Step*. Amnesty International, 1989.

## FICTION BOOKS RELATING TO TOPIC

Capote, Truman. *In Cold Blood*, 1965. (adult)
Gaines, Ernest. *A Lesson before Dying*, 1993. (adult)
Mailer, Norman. *Executioner's Song*, 1979. (adult)

## NATIONAL ORGANIZATIONS TO CONTACT FOR ADDITIONAL INFORMATION

American Civil Liberties Union, Capital Punishment Project, 122 Maryland Ave., N.E., Washington, DC 20002.
Death Penalty Information Center, 1606 20th St., 2nd Fl., Washington, DC 20009.
National Coalition to Abolish the Death Penalty, 1325 G St., N.W., Washington, DC 20005.

## SUGGESTIONS FOR NARROWING THIS TOPIC

Discuss the moral and ethical aspects of the death penalty issue.
Investigate teens and the death penalty.
Is capital punishment a deterrent to crime?
Should executions be televised?

## SUGGESTIONS FOR RELATED TOPICS

Alternatives to capital punishment
Death row and the right to legal representation
Prison reform
Prisoner rehabilitation

This RESEARCH TOPIC GUIDE is intended to help the library user find information and materials on a particular topic in many sources throughout the library. Resources on this topic are not limited to those described and availability will depend upon the individual library. Feel free to ask a librarian for assistance.

# Censorship

**BACKGROUND**

Attempts by government or individuals to ban books, prosecute artists and writers for their work, shut down stores dealing in pornography, and restrict music lyrics are considered by many to be forms of censorship and an abridgement of freedom of speech.

**BROWSE FOR BOOKS ON THE SHELF USING THESE CALL NUMBERS**

> 363.31
> 323.4

**LOOK UNDER THE FOLLOWING SUBJECTS IN THE CATALOG (CARD OR COMPUTER)**

> Censorship
> Censorship—United States
> Freedom of the press
> Freedom of speech

**USE PAMPHLET FILE (ALSO CALLED VERTICAL FILE) UNDER THE HEADING**

> Censorship

**REFERENCE MATERIALS THAT MAY HELP (BOOKS OR CD-ROMS)**

> *CQ Researcher*, February 19, 1993.
> Green, Jonathan, ed. *The Encyclopedia of Censorship,* 1990.
> Hurwitz, Leon, ed. *Historical Dictionary of Censorship in the United States*, 1985.
> General encyclopedias

**PERIODICAL INDEXES TO SEARCH (BOOKS OR CD-ROMS)**

> EBSCO Magazine Article Summaries
> InfoTrac
> NewsBank and other newspaper indexes
> Readers' Guide to Periodical Literature
> SIRS (Social Issues Resources Series)
> WILSONDISC

**ONLINE DATABASES TO SEARCH**

> America Online
> CompuServe
> Dialog
> Internet
> Prodigy

## KEY WORDS AND DESCRIPTORS FOR PERIODICAL INDEX AND ONLINE SEARCHES

Censorship
Condemned books
Freedom of the press
Freedom of speech
Arts—censorship

## VIDEOTAPES ON THIS TOPIC

*Books Our Children Read.* Films, Inc., 1984.
*Damned in the USA.* Gabriel Films, 1992.
*Fahrenheit 451.* MCA Home Video, 1985.

## FICTION BOOKS RELATING TO TOPIC

Bradbury, Ray. *Fahrenheit 451*, 1953.
Hentoff, Nat. *The Day They Came to Arrest the Book*, 1982.
Peck, Richard. *The Last Safe Place on Earth*, 1994.

## NATIONAL ORGANIZATIONS TO CONTACT FOR ADDITIONAL INFORMATION

American Library Association, Freedom to Read Foundation, 50 E. Huron St., Chicago, IL 60011.
National Coalition against Censorship, 2 W. 64th St., New York, NY 10023.
People for the American Way, 2000 M St., N.W., Ste. 400, Washington, DC 20036.

## SUGGESTIONS FOR NARROWING THIS TOPIC

Discuss book censorship in schools and libraries.
Discuss censorship and the Internet.
Investigate censorship on campuses.
Report on a specific censorship incident involving books, art, or music lyrics.
Research talk radio and the censorship issue.

## SUGGESTIONS FOR RELATED TOPICS

Freedom of the press
Movie rating system
Pornography
Rap/Rock music lyrics

This RESEARCH TOPIC GUIDE is intended to help the library user find information and materials on a particular topic in many sources throughout the library. Resources on this topic are not limited to those described and availability will depend upon the individual library. Feel free to ask a librarian for assistance.

# Child Abuse

BACKGROUND

Although the occurrence of child abuse is not a new phenomenon, it has been increasingly reported to the authorities and covered in the press. Emotional, physical, and sexual abuse of children cause lasting damage with which society must deal.

**BROWSE FOR BOOKS ON THE SHELF USING THESE CALL NUMBERS**

> 364.15–364.155
> 362.7–362.76
> 649.153

**LOOK UNDER THE FOLLOWING SUBJECTS IN THE CATALOG (CARD OR COMPUTER)**

> Child abuse
> Child molesting
> Abused children
> Child sexual abuse—United States

**USE PAMPHLET FILE (ALSO CALLED VERTICAL FILE) UNDER THE HEADING**

> Child abuse

**REFERENCE MATERIALS THAT MAY HELP (BOOKS OR CD-ROMS)**

> Clark, Robin E., and Judith Freeman Clark. *The Encyclopedia of Child Abuse*, 1989.
> *CQ Researcher*, January 15, 1993.
> DiCanio, Margaret. *Encyclopedia of Violence*, 1993.
> General encyclopedias

**PERIODICAL INDEXES TO SEARCH (BOOKS OR CD-ROMS)**

> EBSCO Magazine Article Summaries
> InfoTrac
> NewsBank and other newspaper indexes
> Readers' Guide to Periodical Literature
> SIRS (Social Issues Resources Series)
> WILSONDISC

**ONLINE DATABASES TO SEARCH**

> America Online
> CompuServe
> Dialog
> Internet
> Prodigy

# KEY WORDS AND DESCRIPTORS FOR PERIODICAL INDEX AND ONLINE SEARCHES

Child abuse
Abused children
Abusive men
Battered child syndrome
Child molesting
Child pornography
Child sexual abuse

## VIDEOTAPES ON THIS TOPIC

*Child Abuse*. Films for the Humanities and Sciences, 1987.
*No One Saved Dennis*. Films for the Humanities, 1988.
*Scared Silent: Exposing and Ending Child Abuse*. TelEd, 1992.
*Radio Flyer*. Columbia TriStar Home Video, 1992.

## FICTION BOOKS RELATING TO TOPIC

Crutcher, Chris. *Chinese Handcuffs*, 1989.
Mazer, Norma Fox. *Silver*, 1988.
Voigt, Cynthia. *When She Hollers*, 1994.
Woodson, Jacqueline. *I Hadn't Meant to Tell You This*, 1994.

## NATIONAL ORGANIZATIONS TO CONTACT FOR ADDITIONAL INFORMATION

Child Welfare League of America, 440 1st St., N.W., Ste. 310, Washington, DC 20001.
National Committee for the Prevention of Child Abuse, 332 S. Michigan Ave., Ste. 1600, Chicago, IL 60604–4357.

## SUGGESTIONS FOR NARROWING THIS TOPIC

Discuss physical, psychological, or sexual abuse of children; prevention and causes.
Investigate child abuse on the Internet.
Report on a specific child abuse case; e.g., Lisa Steinberg, McMartin Preschool, Michael Jackson.
Research law and legislation pertaining to child abuse.

## SUGGESTIONS FOR RELATED TOPICS

Children as witnesses
Domestic violence
Incest
Pornography
Rights of children and teenagers
Teenage runaways

This RESEARCH TOPIC GUIDE is intended to help the library user find information and materials on a particular topic in many sources throughout the library. Resources on this topic are not limited to those described and availability will depend upon the individual library. Feel free to ask a librarian for assistance.

# Creationism versus Evolution

## BACKGROUND

Fundamentalist religious movements have attempted to introduce the teaching of the biblical explanation of the origin of life into the schools. Known as scientific creationists, they wish to place religious views on an equal footing with the scientific fact of evolution. Controversy over this issue has resulted in litigation involving the Supreme Court.

## BROWSE FOR BOOKS ON THE SHELF USING THESE CALL NUMBERS

> 231.765
> 347.30477–347.30495
> 575–575.016

## LOOK UNDER THE FOLLOWING SUBJECTS IN THE CATALOG (CARD OR COMPUTER)

> Creationism
> Creationism—Controversial literature
> Creationism—Study and teaching
> Creationism—Study and teaching—Law and legislation
> Creation
> Evolution and religion
> Bible and evolution
> Evolution (Biology)—Religious aspects
> Science and law

## REFERENCE MATERIALS THAT MAY HELP (BOOKS OR CD-ROMS)

> Bergman, Jeffrey. *The Creation Evolution Controversy: A Bibliographic Guide from 1839 to the Present*, 1995.
>
> Ecker, Ronald L. *Dictionary of Science and Creationism*, 1990.
>
> *Facts on File*
>
> Hall, Kermit L., ed. *The Oxford Companion to the Supreme Court of the United States*, 1992.
>
> General encyclopedias

## PERIODICAL INDEXES TO SEARCH (BOOKS OR CD-ROMS)

> EBSCO Magazine Article Summaries
> InfoTrac

NewsBank and other newspaper indexes
Readers' Guide to Periodical Literature
SIRS (Social Issues Resources Series)
WILSONDISC

## ONLINE DATABASES TO SEARCH

Dialog

Internet

## KEY WORDS AND DESCRIPTORS FOR PERIODICAL INDEX AND ONLINE SEARCHES

Evolution

Creation

Creationism

Curriculum Programs, Elementary and Secondary—Creation vs. evolution

## VIDEOTAPES ON THIS TOPIC

*Natural Connections*. New Dimensions Media, 1988.

*Origin of Species: Beyond Genesis*. Discovery Communications, 1993.

## NATIONAL ORGANIZATIONS TO CONTACT FOR ADDITIONAL INFORMATION

Creation Research Society, P.O. Box 28473, Kansas City, MO 64118.

National Center for Science Education, 2530 San Pablo Ave., No. D., Berkeley, CA 94702–2013.

## SUGGESTIONS FOR NARROWING THIS TOPIC

Discuss evangelical theology and evolutionary thought.

Investigate how science textbooks deal with the topics of creation and evolution.

Report on a specific case in which creationists challenged evolution in the curriculum; e.g., Little Rock, Arkansas, in 1981.

## SUGGESTIONS FOR RELATED TOPICS

Charles Darwin

Creation myths

Scientific theories of creation

Scopes trial

This RESEARCH TOPIC GUIDE is intended to help the library user find information and materials on a particular topic in many sources throughout the library. Resources on this topic are not limited to those described and availability will depend upon the individual library. Feel free to ask a librarian for assistance.

# Cults

## BACKGROUND

Cults, religious movements that originate outside established denominations, exist in many forms and recruit members using varying tactics. They are often headed by charismatic leaders who are believed to brainwash the cult members into submission.

## BROWSE FOR BOOKS ON THE SHELF USING THESE CALL NUMBERS

291–291.9
133.4
290
362.2

## LOOK UNDER THE FOLLOWING SUBJECTS IN THE CATALOG (CARD OR COMPUTER)

Cults
Cults—United States
Sects

## USE PAMPHLET FILE (ALSO CALLED VERTICAL FILE) UNDER THE HEADING

Cults

## REFERENCE MATERIALS THAT MAY HELP (BOOKS OR CD-ROMS)

Butterworth, John. *Cults and New Faiths: A Book of Beliefs*, 1982.
*CQ Researcher*, May 5, 1993.
*Facts on File*
Melton, J. Gordon. *The Encyclopedia of American Religions*, 1994.
Melton, J. Gordon. *The Encyclopedic Handbook of Cults in America*, 1993.
General encyclopedias

## PERIODICAL INDEXES TO SEARCH (BOOKS OR CD-ROMS)

EBSCO Magazine Article Summaries
InfoTrac
NewsBank and other newspaper indexes
Readers' Guide to Periodical Literature
SIRS (Social Issues Resources Series)
WILSONDISC

## ONLINE DATABASES TO SEARCH

America Online
CompuServe
Dialog
Internet
Prodigy

## KEY WORDS AND DESCRIPTORS FOR PERIODICAL INDEX AND ONLINE SEARCHES

Cults
Sects
Satanism
Christianity and occultism
Christianity and the New Age movement

## VIDEOTAPES ON THIS TOPIC

*The New Believers*. Monticello Productions, 1990.
*The Rapture*. Columbia TriStar Home Video, 1992.

## FICTION BOOKS RELATING TO TOPIC

Nasaw, Jonathan. *Shakedown Street*, 1995.
Slepian, Jan. *Something beyond Paradise*, 1987.
Tolan, Stephanie S. *A Good Courage*, 1988.

## NATIONAL ORGANIZATIONS TO CONTACT FOR ADDITIONAL INFORMATION

American Family Foundation, P.O. Box 6336, Weston, MA 02193.
Cult Awareness Network, 2421 W. Pratt Blvd., Ste. 1173, Chicago, IL 60645.

## SUGGESTIONS FOR NARROWING THIS TOPIC

Report on a specific cult; e.g., Hare Krishna, Unification Church, Branch Davidians.
Discuss recruiting and mind control techniques employed by some cults.
Research ancient cults; e.g., Druids, Apocalyptic cults.
Discuss the moral, ethical, and legal issues surrounding cults and freedom of religion.

## SUGGESTIONS FOR RELATED TOPICS

Deprogramming
New Age movement
Nostradamus
Occultism
Parapsychology
Waco Branch Davidian Disaster

This RESEARCH TOPIC GUIDE is intended to help the library user find information and materials on a particular topic in many sources throughout the library. Resources on this topic are not limited to those described and availability will depend upon the individual library. Feel free to ask a librarian for assistance.

# Drugs and Athletes

## BACKGROUND

Taking steroids to enhance athletic performance has become widespread among athletes worldwide. This practice not only violates athletic regulations and the intent of fair competition but also damages many of the body's major organs.

## BROWSE FOR BOOKS ON THE SHELF USING THESE CALL NUMBERS

362.2–362.293
613.77–613.83
615.7–615.77

## LOOK UNDER THE FOLLOWING SUBJECTS IN THE CATALOG (CARD OR COMPUTER)

Athletes—Drug use
Steroids
Anabolic steroids—Health aspects
Doping in sports

## USE PAMPHLET FILE (ALSO CALLED VERTICAL FILE) UNDER THE HEADINGS

Steroids
Drug abuse—Steroids

## REFERENCE MATERIALS THAT MAY HELP (BOOKS OR CD-ROMS)

*CQ Researcher*, July 26, 1991.
Jaffe, Jerome, ed. *Encyclopedia of Drugs and Alcohol*, 1994.
O'Brien, Robert, et al. *Encyclopedia of Drug Abuse*, 1992.

## PERIODICAL INDEXES TO SEARCH (BOOKS OR CD-ROMS)

EBSCO Magazine Article Summaries
InfoTrac
NewsBank and other newspaper indexes
Readers' Guide to Periodical Literature
SIRS (Social Issues Resources Series)
WILSONDISC

## ONLINE DATABASES TO SEARCH

America Online
CompuServe
Dialog

Internet
Prodigy

## KEY WORDS AND DESCRIPTORS FOR PERIODICAL INDEX AND ONLINE SEARCHES

Drugs and athletes
Drugs and sports
Steroids
Anabolic steroids
Drug use in sports
Drug use and abuse—Steroids

## VIDEOTAPES ON THIS TOPIC

*Anabolic Steroids: Quest for Superman*. Human Relations Media, 1992.
*Downfall, Sports and Drugs*. National Audiovisual Center, 1988.

## FICTION BOOK RELATING TO TOPIC

Miklowitz, Gloria D. *Anything to Win*, 1989.

## NATIONAL ORGANIZATIONS TO CONTACT FOR ADDITIONAL INFORMATION

Drug Information Association, P.O. Box 3113, Maple Glen, PA 19002.
National Collegiate Athletic Association, 6201 College Blvd., Overland Park, KS 66211.
U.S. Olympic Committee, 1750 E. Boulder St., Colorado Springs, CO 80909.

## SUGGESTIONS FOR NARROWING THIS TOPIC

Analyze the pros and cons of the drug testing of athletes.
Discuss drug use among Olympic athletes, professional athletes, college athletes, or body builders.
Discuss policies established by sports governing bodies regarding use of drugs.
Report on the case of an athlete who abused drugs; e.g., Ben Johnson.
What are the adverse effects of steroid use?

## SUGGESTIONS FOR RELATED TOPICS

Nutrition for athletes
Sports medicine
Use of steroids in medicine

This RESEARCH TOPIC GUIDE is intended to help the library user find information and materials on a particular topic in many sources throughout the library. Resources on this topic are not limited to those described and availability will depend upon the individual library. Feel free to ask a librarian for assistance.

# Eating Disorders

**BACKGROUND**

Anorexia, bulimia, and compulsive eating are the major eating disorders with which many people, especially young women, are struggling. Although there is disagreement within the medical community over whether to treat the disorders as psychological or physiological conditions, most doctors and therapists recognize the severity of these life-threatening illnesses.

**BROWSE FOR BOOKS ON THE SHELF USING THESE CALL NUMBERS**

> 616.852–616.8526
> 616.389
> 613.25–613.39

**LOOK UNDER THE FOLLOWING SUBJECTS IN THE CATALOG (CARD OR COMPUTER)**

> Eating disorders
> Anorexia nervosa
> Bulimia
> Compulsive eating

**USE PAMPHLET FILE (ALSO CALLED VERTICAL FILE) UNDER THE HEADING**

> Eating disorders

**REFERENCE MATERIALS THAT MAY HELP (BOOKS OR CD-ROMS)**

> Brownell, Kelly D., et al. *Eating Disorders and Obesity: A Comprehensive Handbook*, 1995.
> Cassell, Dana K., and E. F. Larocca. *The Encyclopedia of Obesity and Eating Disorders*, 1994.
> *CQ Researcher*, December 18, 1992.
> General encyclopedias

**PERIODICAL INDEXES TO SEARCH (BOOKS OR CD-ROMS)**

> EBSCO Magazine Article Summaries
> InfoTrac
> NewsBank and other newspaper indexes
> Readers' Guide to Periodical Literature
> SIRS (Social Issues Resources Series)
> WILSONDISC

**ONLINE DATABASES TO SEARCH**

> America Online
> CompuServe
> Dialog

Internet
Prodigy

## KEY WORDS AND DESCRIPTORS FOR PERIODICAL INDEX AND ONLINE SEARCHES

Eating disorders
Anorexia
Anorexia nervosa
Bulimia
Compulsive eating

## VIDEOTAPES ON THIS TOPIC

*Cathy Rigby: On Eating Disorders*. Increase Video, 1990.
*Eating Disorders*. Films for the Humanities and Sciences, 1990.
*Eating Disorders*. Schlessinger Video Productions, 1994.

## FICTION BOOKS RELATING TO TOPIC

Benning, Elizabeth. *Please Don't Go*, 1993.
Newman, Leslea. *Fat Chance*, 1994.

## NATIONAL ORGANIZATIONS TO CONTACT FOR ADDITIONAL INFORMATION

American Anorexia/Bulimia Association, 418 E. 76th St., New York, NY 10021.
National Anorexic Aid Society, 1925 E. Dublin Rd., Columbus, OH 43229.

## SUGGESTIONS FOR NARROWING THIS TOPIC

Discuss the possible relationship between eating disorders and the cultural view of women.
Investigate the treatment of eating disorders.
Report on a specific eating disorder.
Discuss eating disorders and female athletes.
What causes eating disorders?

## SUGGESTIONS FOR RELATED TOPICS

Body image
Female gymnasts
Modeling industry
Post–traumatic stress disorder

This RESEARCH TOPIC GUIDE is intended to help the library user find information and materials on a particular topic in many sources throughout the library. Resources on this topic are not limited to those described and availability will depend upon the individual library. Feel free to ask a librarian for assistance.

# Fetal Alcohol Syndrome

**BACKGROUND**

Fetal alcohol syndrome is a leading cause of mental retardation. Pregnant women who drink risk damage to the developing fetus from the toxic effects of alcohol in the bloodstream. Retardation ranges from mild to severe depending on the amount of alcohol consumed. Physical deformities can also occur.

**BROWSE FOR BOOKS ON THE SHELF USING THESE CALL NUMBERS**

> 616.861
> 613.81
> 362.29

**LOOK UNDER THE FOLLOWING SUBJECTS IN THE CATALOG (CARD OR COMPUTER)**

> Fetal alcohol syndrome
> Alcoholism—Genetic aspects
> Women—Alcohol use
> Pregnant women—Alcohol use
> Fetus—Effect of drugs on
> Drug abuse in pregnancy

**USE PAMPHLET FILE (ALSO CALLED VERTICAL FILE) UNDER THE HEADINGS**

> Fetal alcohol syndrome
> Alcohol
> Drugs—Alcohol

**REFERENCE MATERIALS THAT MAY HELP (BOOKS OR CD-ROMS)**

> Clayman, Charles B., ed. *The American Medical Association Family Medical Guide*, 1994.
> Jaffe, Jerome, ed. *Encyclopedia of Drugs and Alcohol*, 1994.
> Magalini, Sergio I., et al., eds. *Dictionary of Medical Syndromes*, 1990.
> O'Brien, Robert, and Morris Chafetz, eds. *The Encyclopedia of Alcoholism*, 1991.

**PERIODICAL INDEXES TO SEARCH (BOOKS OR CD-ROMS)**

> EBSCO Magazine Article Summaries
> InfoTrac
> NewsBank and other newspaper indexes

Readers' Guide to Periodical Literature
SIRS (Social Issues Resources Series)
WILSONDISC

## ONLINE DATABASES TO SEARCH

America Online
CompuServe
Dialog
Internet
Prodigy

## KEY WORDS AND DESCRIPTORS FOR PERIODICAL INDEX AND ONLINE SEARCHES

Fetal alcohol syndrome
Fetus—effect of alcohol on
Alcoholism—fetal alcohol syndrome
Pregnant women and alcohol

## NATIONAL ORGANIZATIONS TO CONTACT FOR ADDITIONAL INFORMATION

Alcohol Research Information Service, 1106 E. Oakland St., Lansing, MI 48906.
Mental Retardation Association of America, 211 E. 300 South, Ste. 212, Salt Lake City, UT 84111.

## SUGGESTIONS FOR NARROWING THIS TOPIC

Discuss the high occurrence of fetal alcohol syndrome among Native Americans.
Report on the effects of alcohol on fetal development.
Research birth defects caused by fetal alcohol syndrome.
What kinds of programs are dealing with prevention of fetal alcohol syndrome?

## SUGGESTIONS FOR RELATED TOPICS

Crack babies
Drugs and pregnancy
Fetal rights
Thalidomide

This RESEARCH TOPIC GUIDE is intended to help the library user find information and materials on a particular topic in many sources throughout the library. Resources on this topic are not limited to those described and availability will depend upon the individual library. Feel free to ask a librarian for assistance.

# Gambling—Moral and Ethical Aspects

**BACKGROUND**

At the end of the twentieth century, gambling is widely accepted and available in many locations of the United States. Government lotteries, casino and riverboat gambling, horse and dog racing, and the recent growth of Native American casinos have all contributed to the spread of gambling fever. Still, debate continues over the moral and ethical aspects of this national pastime.

**BROWSE FOR BOOKS ON THE SHELF USING THESE CALL NUMBERS**

> 362.25
> 364.172
> 363.42
> 795.01

**LOOK UNDER THE FOLLOWING SUBJECTS IN THE CATALOG (CARD OR COMPUTER)**

> Compulsive gambling
> Compulsive gamblers
> Compulsive behavior
> Gambling

**USE PAMPHLET FILE (ALSO CALLED VERTICAL FILE) UNDER THE HEADING**

> Gambling

**REFERENCE MATERIALS THAT MAY HELP (BOOKS OR CD-ROMS)**

> *CQ Researcher*, March 18, 1994.
> Galski, Thomas, ed. *The Handbook of Pathological Gambling*, 1987.

**PERIODICAL INDEXES TO SEARCH (BOOKS OR CD-ROMS)**

> EBSCO Magazine Article Summaries
> InfoTrac
> NewsBank and other newspaper indexes
> Readers' Guide to Periodical Literature
> WILSONDISC

**ONLINE DATABASES TO SEARCH**

> America Online
> CompuServe

Dialog
Internet
Prodigy

## KEY WORDS AND DESCRIPTORS FOR PERIODICAL INDEX AND ONLINE SEARCHES

Gambling—moral and religious aspects
Compulsive gambling
Mental health and mental illness—gambling
Casinos
Gambling
Lotteries

## FICTION BOOK RELATING TO TOPIC

Dygard, Thomas J. *Point Spread*, 1980.

## NATIONAL ORGANIZATIONS TO CONTACT FOR ADDITIONAL INFORMATION

Gamblers Anonymous, P.O. Box 17173, Los Angeles, CA 90010.
National Council on Problem Gambling, John Jay College of Criminal Justice, 445 W. 59th St., New York, NY 10019.

## SUGGESTIONS FOR NARROWING THIS TOPIC

Discuss the problem of compulsive gambling.
Investigate the impact of Native American casinos on the problem on compulsive gambling.
Research the possible connection between organized crime and gambling.
Should governments be in the gambling business?

## SUGGESTIONS FOR RELATED TOPICS

Discuss gambling as an economic remedy.
Trace the history of gambling in the United States.
Research a particular casino or resort; e.g., Foxwoods, Atlantic City, Las Vegas.

This RESEARCH TOPIC GUIDE is intended to help the library user find information and materials on a particular topic in many sources throughout the library. Resources on this topic are not limited to those described and availability will depend upon the individual library. Feel free to ask a librarian for assistance.

# Gays in the Military

## BACKGROUND

When President Clinton in 1991 called for the end of the ban on gays in the military, he set off a national debate on the topic that has not been resolved. Some argue that the presence of gays will negatively affect morale and discipline in the military; others feel gays are already serving their country effectively and discrimination against them is unconstitutional.

## BROWSE FOR BOOKS ON THE SHELF USING THESE CALL NUMBERS

    306.766
    355.0086

## LOOK UNDER THE FOLLOWING SUBJECTS IN THE CATALOG (CARD OR COMPUTER)

    United States—Armed Forces—Gays—History—20th century
    United States. Navy—Gays
    United States—Armed Forces—Gays
    United States—Armed Forces—Gays—Legal status, laws, etc.

## REFERENCE MATERIALS THAT MAY HELP (BOOKS OR CD-ROMS)

    *Congressional Quarterly Weekly Report*
    *CQ Almanac*
    *Editorials on File*. Facts on File.
    *Facts on File*

## PERIODICAL INDEXES TO SEARCH (BOOKS OR CD-ROMS)

    EBSCO Magazine Article Summaries
    InfoTrac
    NewsBank and other newspaper indexes
    Readers' Guide to Periodical Literature
    SIRS (Social Issues Resources Series)
    WILSONDISC

## ONLINE DATABASES TO SEARCH

    America Online
    CompuServe

Dialog

Internet

Prodigy

## KEY WORDS AND DESCRIPTORS FOR PERIODICAL INDEX AND ONLINE SEARCHES

Gays in the military

Homosexuals in the military

Gay military personnel

United States—Armed forces—Homosexuals

United States—Armed forces—Gays

United States—Army—Homosexuals

United States—Army—Gays

United States—Navy—Homosexuals

United States—Navy—Gays

## SUGGESTIONS FOR NARROWING THIS TOPIC

Discuss the "Don't ask, don't tell" policy.

Present the case for (or against) gays in the military.

Report on a specific case involving gays in the military; e.g., Tracy Thorne, Margarethe Cammermeyer, Jose Zuniga.

## SUGGESTIONS FOR RELATED TOPICS

Gay rights

Homophobia

Right of privacy

Tailhook Scandal

Women in combat

This RESEARCH TOPIC GUIDE is intended to help the library user find information and materials on a particular topic in many sources throughout the library. Resources on this topic are not limited to those described and availability will depend upon the individual library. Feel free to ask a librarian for assistance.

# Generation X

## BACKGROUND

Generation X, a term coined by novelist Douglas Coupland, refers to the over 44 million people born between 1965 and 1975. This group has been stereotyped by some as unfocused, without ambition, and underachieving. But proponents credit Generation Xers with global awareness and computer skills that should serve them well in today's workplace. Others reject the whole notion that a Generation X exists at all.

## BROWSE FOR BOOKS ON THE SHELF USING THIS CALL NUMBER

305.2350

## LOOK UNDER THE FOLLOWING SUBJECTS IN THE CATALOG (CARD OR COMPUTER)

Mass media and youth—United States

Popular culture—United States

Youth movement

Young adults

## REFERENCE MATERIALS THAT MAY HELP (BOOKS OR CD-ROMS)

*Facts on File*

Mitchell, Susan. *The Official Guide to the Generations*, 1995.

## PERIODICAL INDEXES TO SEARCH (BOOKS OR CD-ROMS)

EBSCO Magazine Article Summaries

InfoTrac

NewsBank and other newspaper indexes

Readers' Guide to Periodical Literature

SIRS (Social Issues Resources Series)

WILSONDISC

## ONLINE DATABASES TO SEARCH

America Online

CompuServe

Dialog

Internet

Prodigy

## KEY WORDS AND DESCRIPTORS FOR PERIODICAL INDEX AND ONLINE SEARCHES

Generation X

Post–Baby Boom generation

Youth

## VIDEOTAPE ON THIS TOPIC

*Where Is My Future? Generation X*. Filmakers Library, 1995.

## FICTION BOOKS RELATING TO TOPIC

Coupland, Douglas. *Generation X: Tales for an Accelerated Culture*, 1991.

Wexler, Michael, and John Hulme, ed. *Voices of the Xiled: A Generation Speaks for Itself*, 1994.

## SUGGESTIONS FOR NARROWING THIS TOPIC

Discuss the attitudes, music, politics, or social behavior of Generation X.

Does Generation X really exist?

Investigate the advertising industry's efforts to target Generation X.

## SUGGESTIONS FOR RELATED TOPICS

Baby Boomers

Coming of age

Generation gap

Woodstock Generation

This RESEARCH TOPIC GUIDE is intended to help the library user find information and materials on a particular topic in many sources throughout the library. Resources on this topic are not limited to those described and availability will depend upon the individual library. Feel free to ask a librarian for assistance.

# Glass Ceiling

## BACKGROUND

Women and minorities encounter invisible barriers to promotion and are often prevented from obtaining business leadership positions. The small percentage of women and minority chief executive officers and board members attests to the fact that there may be such a barrier, a so-called glass ceiling, at the top of the corporate ladder.

## BROWSE FOR BOOKS ON THE SHELF USING THESE CALL NUMBERS

> 331.4
> 305.4
> 301.4
> 658.409

## LOOK UNDER THE FOLLOWING SUBJECTS IN THE CATALOG (CARD OR COMPUTER)

> Women executives—United States
> Discrimination in employment
> Sex discrimination in employment—United States
> Sex roles in the work environment
> Women—Employment—United States

## REFERENCE MATERIALS THAT MAY HELP (BOOKS OR CD-ROMS)

> *CQ Almanac*
> *CQ Researcher*, October 29, 1993.
> *Editorials on File*, Facts on File.
> *Facts on File*
> Trager, Oliver, ed. *Sexual Politics in America*, 1994.

## PERIODICAL INDEXES TO SEARCH (BOOKS OR CD-ROMS)

> EBSCO Magazine Article Summaries
> InfoTrac
> NewsBank and other newspaper indexes
> Readers' Guide to Periodical Literature
> SIRS (Social Issues Resources Series)
> WILSONDISC

## ONLINE DATABASES TO SEARCH

> America Online
> CompuServe

Dialog
Internet
Prodigy

## KEY WORDS AND DESCRIPTORS FOR PERIODICAL INDEX AND ONLINE SEARCHES

Glass ceiling
Discrimination in employment
Working women
Women executives
Women in the workforce
Sex discrimination against women

## NATIONAL ORGANIZATIONS TO CONTACT FOR ADDITIONAL INFORMATION

National Federation of Business and Professional Women's Clubs, Inc., 2012 Massachusetts Ave., N.W., Washington, DC 20036.

U.S. Glass Ceiling Commission, Department of Labor, C/O Women's Bureau, 200 Constitution Ave., N.W., Washington, DC 20036.

## SUGGESTIONS FOR NARROWING THIS TOPIC

Discuss ways in which women are prevented from advancing in employment.
Discuss women clergy and the "stained glass ceiling."
Investigate the findings of the Glass Ceiling Commission (1991).

## SUGGESTIONS FOR RELATED TOPICS

Affirmative action programs
Age discrimination in employment
Equal pay for equal work
Sexual harassment
Women's rights movement

This RESEARCH TOPIC GUIDE is intended to help the library user find information and materials on a particular topic in many sources throughout the library. Resources on this topic are not limited to those described and availability will depend upon the individual library. Feel free to ask a librarian for assistance.

# Gun Control

**BACKGROUND**

With the increase in gun-related crimes, debate over the licensing and control of firearms in the United States continues among the public and in all levels of government. Opinions vary on the constitutionality and effectiveness of restricting gun ownership.

**BROWSE FOR BOOKS ON THE SHELF USING THESE CALL NUMBERS**

> 363.33–363.3309
> 344.73

**LOOK UNDER THE FOLLOWING SUBJECTS IN THE CATALOG (CARD OR COMPUTER)**

> Gun control—United States
> Firearms—Law and legislation—United States

**USE PAMPHLET FILE (ALSO CALLED VERTICAL FILE) UNDER THE HEADING**

> Gun control

**REFERENCE MATERIALS THAT MAY HELP (BOOKS OR CD-ROMS)**

> *CQ Almanac*
> *CQ Researcher*, March 22, 1992, June 10, 1994.
> *Congressional Quarterly Weekly Report.*
> General encyclopedias

**PERIODICAL INDEXES TO SEARCH (BOOKS OR CD-ROMS)**

> EBSCO Magazine Article Summaries
> InfoTrac
> NewsBank and other newspaper indexes
> Readers' Guide to Periodical Literature
> SIRS (Social Issues Resources Series)
> WILSONDISC

**ONLINE DATABASES TO SEARCH**

> America Online
> CompuServe
> Dialog
> Internet
> Prodigy

## KEY WORDS AND DESCRIPTORS FOR PERIODICAL INDEX AND ONLINE SEARCHES

Gun control
Guns and gun control
Firearms
Firearms—laws, regulations, etc.
Right to bear arms

## VIDEOTAPES ON THIS TOPIC

*Gun Control.* National Institute of Justice, 1985.
*What's the Common Ground on Gun Control?* Common Ground–WNYC Productions, 1989.

## FICTION BOOKS RELATING TO TOPIC

Arrick, Fran. *Where'd You Get Your Gun, Billy?* 1991.
Paulsen, Gary. *The Rifle*, 1995.

## NATIONAL ORGANIZATIONS TO CONTACT FOR ADDITIONAL INFORMATION

Coalition to Stop Gun Violence, 100 Maryland Ave., N.E., Washington, DC 20002.
National Rifle Association of America, 1600 Rhode Island Ave., N.W., Washington, DC 20036.

## SUGGESTIONS FOR NARROWING THIS TOPIC

Discuss the Brady Law (1994) or the Clinton Crime Bill (1994) as it pertains to gun control.
Discuss possible effects of a ban on assault weapons or handguns.
Investigate gun control laws in New Jersey, California, Connecticut, or any other state.
Present the case for (or against) gun control.

## SUGGESTIONS FOR RELATED TOPICS

Crime prevention
Gun control in other countries
Gun use in accidental deaths; in homicides
Historical role of guns in the United States
National Rifle Association of America

This RESEARCH TOPIC GUIDE is intended to help the library user find information and materials on a particular topic in many sources throughout the library. Resources on this topic are not limited to those described and availability will depend upon the individual library. Feel free to ask a librarian for assistance.

# Hate Crimes

## BACKGROUND

Hate crimes are those committed against a targeted minority (gays, blacks, Jews, etc.) by a person or group dedicated to promoting hatred and violence. There has been an increase in hate crimes on college campuses as well as in other areas around the country. Experts differ on methods of preventing and dealing with this ugly behavior.

## BROWSE FOR BOOKS ON THE SHELF USING THESE CALL NUMBERS

364.1–364.1523
305.8

## LOOK UNDER THE FOLLOWING SUBJECTS IN THE CATALOG (CARD OR COMPUTER)

Hate crimes
Minorities—Crimes against—United States
Prejudices
Racism—United States

## REFERENCE MATERIALS THAT MAY HELP (BOOKS OR CD-ROMS)

*CQ Researcher*, January 8, 1993.
*Editorials on File*, Facts on File.
*Facts on File*
Freeman, Steven M. *Hate Crimes Laws: A Comprehensive Guide*, 1994.

## PERIODICAL INDEXES TO SEARCH (BOOKS OR CD-ROMS)

EBSCO Magazine Article Summaries
InfoTrac
NewsBank and other newspaper indexes
Readers' Guide to Periodical Literature
SIRS (Social Issues Resources Series)
WILSONDISC

## ONLINE DATABASES TO SEARCH

America Online
CompuServe
Dialog
Internet
Prodigy

## KEY WORDS AND DESCRIPTORS FOR PERIODICAL INDEX AND ONLINE SEARCHES

Hate crimes
Bias assaults

Minorities—crimes against
African Americans—crimes against
Gays—crimes against
Gay persons—hate crimes
Jewish people—hate crimes
Neo-Nazis
Skinheads
White supremacy movements

## VIDEOTAPES ON THIS TOPIC

*Beyond Hate*. Mystic Fire Video, 1991.
*Crimes of Hate*. ADL Film Library, 1990.
*Hate on Trial with Bill Moyers*, Mystic Fire Video, 1992.
*The Klan: A Legacy of Hate in America*. Films, Inc., 1989.
*Mississippi Burning*. Orion Home Video, 1988.

## FICTION BOOKS RELATING TO TOPIC

Greene, Bette. *The Drowning of Stephen Jones*, 1991.
Taylor, Mildred D. *The Road to Memphis*, 1990.

## NATIONAL ORGANIZATIONS TO CONTACT FOR ADDITIONAL INFORMATION

American Civil Liberties Union, 132 W. 43rd St., New York, NY 10036.
Anti-Defamation League, 823 UN Plaza, New York, NY 10017.
National Institute against Prejudice and Violence, 31 S. Greene St., Baltimore, MD 21201.

## SUGGESTIONS FOR NARROWING THIS TOPIC

Discuss hate crimes as they relate to the First Amendment to the Constitution.
Discuss the rise of white supremacy movements; e.g., Neo-Nazis, Aryan Nations, Skin Heads.
Investigate hate crimes on campus.
Research hate crime legislation.

## SUGGESTIONS FOR RELATED TOPICS

Anti-Semitism
Extremist groups in the United States
Hate speech
Holocaust
Racism
Stalking
Talk radio

This RESEARCH TOPIC GUIDE is intended to help the library user find information and materials on a particular topic in many sources throughout the library. Resources on this topic are not limited to those described and availability will depend upon the individual library. Feel free to ask a librarian for assistance.

# Home Schooling

## BACKGROUND

Home schooling is a growing trend in the United States. Reasons for this phenomenon include the perception that the quality of education is declining, violence and drugs in the schools, and a desire to include religion in the curriculum. The pros and cons of the home schooling movement continue to be debated.

## BROWSE FOR BOOKS ON THE SHELF USING THESE CALL NUMBERS

370.1
371–371.394
649.1–649.124

## LOOK UNDER THE FOLLOWING SUBJECTS IN THE CATALOG (CARD OR COMPUTER)

Home schooling
Education—Parent participation
Domestic education

## USE PAMPHLET FILE (ALSO CALLED VERTICAL FILE) UNDER THE HEADINGS

Home schooling
Education—Home schooling

## REFERENCE MATERIALS THAT MAY HELP (BOOKS OR CD-ROMS)

*CQ Researcher*, September 9, 1994.
Brostrom, David C. *A Guide to Homeschooling for Librarians*, 1995.
Hood, Mary. *Home Schooling Resource Guide and Directory of Organizations*, 1993.
Mintz, Jerry, ed. *The Almanac of Education Choices: Private and Public Learning Alternatives*, 1995.

## PERIODICAL INDEXES TO SEARCH (BOOKS OR CD-ROMS)

EBSCO Magazine Article Summaries
InfoTrac
NewsBank and other newspaper indexes
Readers' Guide to Periodical Literature
SIRS (Social Issues Resources Series)
WILSONDISC

## ONLINE DATABASES TO SEARCH

America Online
CompuServe
Dialog
Internet
Prodigy

## KEY WORDS AND DESCRIPTORS FOR PERIODICAL INDEX AND ONLINE SEARCHES

Home school (also homeschool)
Home schoolers (also homeschoolers)
Home schooling (also homeschooling)
Home education

## NATIONAL ORGANIZATIONS TO CONTACT FOR ADDITIONAL INFORMATION

Home School Legal Defense Association, P.O. Box 159, Paeonian Springs, VA 22129.
National Homeschool Association, P.O. Box 290, Hartland, MI 48353–0290.

## SUGGESTIONS FOR NARROWING THIS TOPIC

Discuss home schooling as it relates to religion.
Discuss home schooling of gifted children; of disabled children.
Evaluate the pros and cons of home schooling.
Look into the new phenomenon of online homeschooling.
Research the home schooling laws and regulations in one or more states.

## SUGGESTIONS FOR RELATED TOPICS

Church schools
Colonial education in the United States
Montessori schools
Parental participation in education

This RESEARCH TOPIC GUIDE is intended to help the library user find information and materials on a particular topic in many sources throughout the library. Resources on this topic are not limited to those described and availability will depend upon the individual library. Feel free to ask a librarian for assistance.

# The Homeless

## BACKGROUND

The problem of homelessness is glaringly evident in all large cities as well as most other areas in the United States. Causes of homelessness are related to the economy, mental illness, and drug addiction, among others. Solutions are debated in newspapers, on television talk shows, and in the United States Congress.

## BROWSE FOR BOOKS ON THE SHELF USING THESE CALL NUMBERS

362.2
362.5–362.58
362.708–362.83
305.568

## LOOK UNDER THE FOLLOWING SUBJECTS IN THE CATALOG (CARD OR COMPUTER)

Homeless persons
Homeless persons—United States
Homelessness

## USE PAMPHLET FILE (ALSO CALLED VERTICAL FILE) UNDER THE HEADINGS

homeless
homelessness

## REFERENCE MATERIALS THAT MAY HELP (BOOKS OR CD-ROMS)

*CQ Researcher*, August 7, 1992.
Goodnight, Lynn, and Arnie Madsen. *Helping the Homeless*, 1991.
Henslin, James M. *Homelessness: An Annotated Bibliography*, 1993.
Hombs, Mary Ellen. *American Homelessness: A Reference Handbook*, 1994.

## PERIODICAL INDEXES TO SEARCH (BOOKS OR CD-ROMS)

EBSCO Magazine Article Summaries
InfoTrac
NewsBank
Readers' Guide to Periodical Literature
SIRS (Social Issues Resources Series)
WILSONDISC

## ONLINE DATABASES TO SEARCH

America Online
CompuServe
Dialog
Internet
Prodigy

## KEY WORDS AND DESCRIPTORS FOR PERIODICAL INDEX AND ONLINE SEARCHES

Homeless
Homeless persons
Homelessness
Homeless children
Homeless families
Homeless women
Homeless youth
Runaways

## VIDEOTAPES ON THIS TOPIC

*Down and Out in America*. MPI Home Video, 1987.
*Fisher King*. Columbia TriStar Home Video, 1991.
*A Place Called Home*. PBS Video, 1989.
*Saint of Fort Washington*. Warner Home Video, 1994.

## FICTION BOOKS RELATING TO TOPIC

Harris, Mark Jonathan. *Come the Morning*, 1989.
Jones, Adrienne. *Street Family*, 1987.
Spinelli, Jerry. *Maniac Magee*, 1990.

## NATIONAL ORGANIZATIONS TO CONTACT FOR ADDITIONAL INFORMATION

National Alliance to End Homelessness, 1518 K St., N.W., Ste. 206, Washington, DC 20005.
National Coalition for the Homeless, 1621 Connecticut Ave., N.W., No. 400, Washington, DC 20009.

## SUGGESTIONS FOR NARROWING THIS TOPIC

Discuss the situation of homeless children.
Evaluate the causes of (or solutions to) homelessness.
Investigate laws concerning the homeless.
Report on a homeless shelter in or near your town.
Research homelessness during the Great Depression of the 1930s.

## SUGGESTIONS FOR RELATED TOPICS

Deinstitutionalism of the mentally ill
Orphanages
Panhandling
Runaway teenagers
Squatters

This RESEARCH TOPIC GUIDE is intended to help the library user find information and materials on a particular topic in many sources throughout the library. Resources on this topic are not limited to those described and availability will depend upon the individual library. Feel free to ask a librarian for assistance.

# Hunting

**BACKGROUND**

Hunting has been a part of America's history from its earliest beginnings and once provided a necessary source of food. Now, no longer needed for subsistence, hunting has evolved as a popular pastime. Opponents of sports hunting, who condemn the unnecessary killing of wildlife, have become increasingly outspoken, causing the hunters to organize powerful lobbying groups.

**BROWSE FOR BOOKS ON THE SHELF USING THESE CALL NUMBERS**

> 174.3
> 179.3
> 799.2

**LOOK UNDER THE FOLLOWING SUBJECTS IN THE CATALOG (CARD OR COMPUTER)**

> Hunting—moral and ethical aspects
> Hunting—moral and religious aspects

**USE PAMPHLET FILE (ALSO CALLED VERTICAL FILE) UNDER THE HEADINGS**

> Animal welfare
> Hunting

**REFERENCE MATERIALS THAT MAY HELP (BOOKS OR CD-ROMS)**

> *CQ Researcher*, January 24, 1992.
> *Editorials on File*. Facts on File.
> Seredich, John, ed. *Your Resource Guide to Environmental Organizations*, 1991.
> General encyclopedias

**PERIODICAL INDEXES TO SEARCH (BOOKS OR CD-ROMS)**

> EBSCO Magazine Article Summaries
> InfoTrac
> NewsBank and other newspaper indexes
> Readers' Guide to Periodical Literature
> SIRS (Social Issues Resources Series)
> WILSONDISC

**ONLINE DATABASES TO SEARCH**

> America Online
> CompuServe
> Dialog

Internet

Prodigy

## KEY WORDS AND DESCRIPTORS FOR PERIODICAL INDEX AND ONLINE SEARCHES

Hunting—moral and ethical aspects

Hunting—public opinion

Sports, Amateur—hunting

Wildlife conservation

Wildlife management

## VIDEOTAPE ON THIS TOPIC

*Wildlife Conservation and the Hunting Tradition*. University of Montana, 1992.

## FICTION BOOKS RELATING TO TOPIC

Hughes, Monica. *Hunter in the Dark*, 1982.

Paulsen, Gary. *Tracker*, 1984.

## NATIONAL ORGANIZATIONS TO CONTACT FOR ADDITIONAL INFORMATION

Committee to Abolish Sport Hunting, P.O. Box 43, White Plains, NY 10605.

National Rifle Association, 1600 Rhode Island Ave., N.W., Washington, DC 20036.

## SUGGESTIONS FOR NARROWING THIS TOPIC

Describe a safari and discuss impact on the environment.

Discuss the impact of hunting on the American bison and the passenger pigeon.

Evaluate the impact of hunting on the environment.

Investigate the wildlife management aspects of hunting.

## SUGGESTIONS FOR RELATED TOPICS

Hunting lobby

Poaching

Reintroduction of the wolf in Minnesota and elsewhere.

Wildlife law

Wildlife refuges

This RESEARCH TOPIC GUIDE is intended to help the library user find information and materials on a particular topic in many sources throughout the library. Resources on this topic are not limited to those described and availability will depend upon the individual library. Feel free to ask a librarian for assistance.

# Learning Disabilities

## BACKGROUND

Over 2 million children in the United States have learning disabilities that impair their ability to succeed in school. No less intelligent than their peers, these students need special services to help them compensate and learn survival skills.

## BROWSE FOR BOOKS ON THE SHELF USING THESE CALL NUMBERS

371.9
370.152
616.89
618.928
649.15

## LOOK UNDER THE FOLLOWING SUBJECTS IN THE CATALOG (CARD OR COMPUTER)

Learning disabilities
Learning disabled children
Learning disabled children—Education
Use heading for specific learning disability; e.g., dyslexia, attention deficit disorder (ADD)

## USE PAMPHLET FILE (ALSO CALLED VERTICAL FILE) UNDER THE HEADINGS

Learning disabilities
Special education

## REFERENCE MATERIALS THAT MAY HELP (BOOKS OR CD-ROMS)

Breakstone, David R., et al., eds. *The New Child Health Encyclopedia*, 1987.
Corsini, Raymond J., ed. *Encyclopedia of Psychology*, 1994.
*CQ Researcher*, December 10, 1993.
*Facts on File*
General encyclopedias

## PERIODICAL INDEXES TO SEARCH (BOOKS OR CD-ROMS)

EBSCO Magazine Article Summaries
InfoTrac
NewsBank and other newspaper indexes
Readers' Guide to Periodical Literature
SIRS (Social Issues Resources Series)
WILSONDISC

## ONLINE DATABASES TO SEARCH

America Online
CompuServe

Dialog

Internet

Prodigy

# KEY WORDS AND DESCRIPTORS FOR PERIODICAL INDEX AND ONLINE SEARCHES

Learning disabilities

Learning disabled children

Reading disability

Special education—learning disabled

Attention deficit disorder (also ADD)

Dyslexia

# VIDEOTAPES ON THIS TOPIC

*ABC's of ADD*. JKL Communications, 1993.

*Adults with Attention Deficit Disorder*. Child Management, 1994.

# FICTION BOOKS RELATING TO TOPIC

Brown, Kay. *Willy's Summer Dream*, 1989.

Hall, Lynn. *Just One Friend*, 1988.

Wolff, Virginia. *Probably Still Nick Swansen*, 1988.

# NATIONAL ORGANIZATION TO CONTACT FOR ADDITIONAL INFORMATION

Learning Disabilities Association of America, 4156 Library Rd., Pittsburgh, PA 15234.

# SUGGESTIONS FOR NARROWING THIS TOPIC

Discuss the laws and regulations regarding the rights of those with learning disorders.

Investigate drug and/or nutritional treatment of learning disorders.

Report on a specific learning disability; e.g., dyslexia, attention deficit disorder (ADD).

What are the genetic aspects of learning disorders?

What are some of the psychological effects of having a learning disability?

# SUGGESTIONS FOR RELATED TOPICS

Americans with Disabilities Act

Behavior modification

Gifted children

Special education

This RESEARCH TOPIC GUIDE is intended to help the library user find information and materials on a particular topic in many sources throughout the library. Resources on this topic are not limited to those described and availability will depend upon the individual library. Feel free to ask a librarian for assistance.

# Legal Rights of Teenagers

## BACKGROUND

American teenagers have more legal rights today than ever before. These rights apply to all areas of their lives, including, but not limited to, school, employment, home, sex, personal appearance, and marriage. To be truly empowered, teenagers need to know and understand their rights under the law.

## BROWSE FOR BOOKS ON THE SHELF USING THESE CALL NUMBERS

> 346.73–346.7301
> 346.012
> 346.7301
> 347.30479
> 305.23

## LOOK UNDER THE FOLLOWING SUBJECTS IN THE CATALOG (CARD OR COMPUTER)

> Youth—Legal status, laws, etc.—United States
> Children—Legal status, laws, etc.—United States
> Students—Legal status, laws, etc.—United States
> Children's rights
> Children's rights—United States

## REFERENCE MATERIALS THAT MAY HELP (BOOKS OR CD-ROMS)

*CQ Researcher*, April 23, 1993.

Hempelman, Kathleen. *Teen Legal Rights: A Guide for the '90s,* 1994.

Price, Janet R., et al. *The Rights of Students: The Basic ACLU Guide to a Student's Rights*, 1988.

Weeks, J. Devereux. *Student Rights under the Constitution*, 1992.

## PERIODICAL INDEXES TO SEARCH (BOOKS OR CD-ROMS)

EBSCO Magazine Article Summaries
InfoTrac
NewsBank and other newspaper indexes
Readers' Guide to Periodical Literature
SIRS (Social Issues Resources Series)
WILSONDISC

## ONLINE DATABASES TO SEARCH

America Online
CompuServe

Dialog
Internet
Prodigy

## KEY WORDS AND DESCRIPTORS FOR PERIODICAL INDEX AND ONLINE SEARCHES

Teenagers' rights
Children's rights
Teenagers—laws, regulations
Children—civil rights
Civil liberties and teenagers
Youth lawsuits

## FICTION BOOK RELATING TO TOPIC

Korczak, Janusz. *King Matt the First*, 1986.

## NATIONAL ORGANIZATIONS TO CONTACT FOR ADDITIONAL INFORMATION

American Civil Liberties Union, 132 W. 43rd St., New York, NY 10036.
National Center for Youth Law, 1663 Mission St., 5th Fl., San Francisco, CA 94103.

## SUGGESTIONS FOR NARROWING THIS TOPIC

Are dress codes in the public schools constitutional?
Discuss teenagers' rights to privacy.
Investigate children divorcing parents.
Report on discrimination against teens.

## SUGGESTIONS FOR RELATED TOPICS

Children's rights movement
Censorship
Marion Wright Edelman
Parental kidnapping
Public school law—teachers' and students' rights

This RESEARCH TOPIC GUIDE is intended to help the library user find information and materials on a particular topic in many sources throughout the library. Resources on this topic are not limited to those described and availability will depend upon the individual library. Feel free to ask a librarian for assistance.

# Medical Ethics

**BACKGROUND**

With the incredible advances in medical research during the twentieth century, scientists are able to cure many diseases, operate on unborn fetuses, produce test tube babies, and transplant almost any organ. But what *can* be done and what *should* be done are totally different concepts. Most agree that scientific knowledge must be tempered with wisdom. Public debate over who should make these important decisions continues.

**BROWSE FOR BOOKS ON THE SHELF USING THESE CALL NUMBERS**

> 174.2—174.22
> 616—616.042
> 362.1

**LOOK UNDER THE FOLLOWING SUBJECTS IN THE CATALOG (CARD OR COMPUTER)**

> Medical ethics
> Bioethics
> Medicine—Decision making
> Ethics, Medical

**REFERENCE MATERIALS THAT MAY HELP (BOOKS OR CD-ROMS)**

> Dunstan, Duncan, et al., eds. *Dictionary of Medical Ethics*, 1981.
> Reich, Warren T., ed. *Encyclopedia of Bioethics*, 1995.
> Walters, Leroy, and Tamar Joy Kahn. *Bibliography of Bioethics*, 1994.

**PERIODICAL INDEXES TO SEARCH (BOOKS OR CD-ROMS)**

> EBSCO Magazine Article Summaries
> InfoTrac
> NewsBank and other newspaper indexes
> Readers' Guide to Periodical Literature
> SIRS (Social Issues Resources Series)
> WILSONDISC

**ONLINE DATABASES TO SEARCH**

> America Online
> CompuServe

Dialog
Internet
Prodigy

## KEY WORDS AND DESCRIPTORS FOR PERIODICAL INDEX AND ONLINE SEARCHES

Medical ethics
Bioethics
Ethics in medicine

## VIDEOTAPES ON THIS TOPIC

*Deadly Deception.* Films for the Humanities and Sciences, 1993.
*Right to Die: Final Choices.* Health and Science Television Network, 1992.

## NATIONAL ORGANIZATIONS TO CONTACT FOR ADDITIONAL INFORMATION

American Medical Association, 535 N. Dearborn St., Chicago, IL 60610.
Council for Responsible Genetics, 19 Garden St., Cambridge, MA 02138.

## SUGGESTIONS FOR NARROWING THIS TOPIC

Discuss the use of technology to save lives of the terminally ill.
Investigate the use of genetic counseling.
Research the issue of allocation of scarce resources; e.g., organs for transplantation, rare blood types, drugs in short supply.

## SUGGESTIONS FOR RELATED TOPICS

Abortion
Assisted suicide
Euthanasia
Genetic engineering
Health insurance

This RESEARCH TOPIC GUIDE is intended to help the library user find information and materials on a particular topic in many sources throughout the library. Resources on this topic are not limited to those described and availability will depend upon the individual library. Feel free to ask a librarian for assistance.

# Near-Death Experiences

## BACKGROUND

Throughout history there have been reports of near-death experiences by people who have had close calls with death. They claim to have experienced one or more of a variety of mystical phenomena; for example, rushing through a dark tunnel toward a brilliant light, observing themselves dying from an out-of-body location, feeling a sense of peace and joy. Since near-death experiences have yet to be authenticated by medical science, they are still generally considered to be in the realm of parapsychology.

## BROWSE FOR BOOKS ON THE SHELF USING THESE CALL NUMBERS

133.9–133.9013
155.937
001.942

## LOOK UNDER THE FOLLOWING SUBJECTS IN THE CATALOG (CARD OR COMPUTER)

Near-death experiences
Near-death experiences—Case studies
Near-death experiences—Psychological aspects
Near-death experiences—Religious aspects
Death—Psychological aspects
Death, Apparent

## REFERENCE MATERIALS THAT MAY HELP (BOOKS OR CD-ROMS)

Basford, Terry K. *Near-Death Experiences: An Annotated Bibliography*, 1990.

Guiley, Rosemary Ellen. *Harper's Encyclopedia of Mystical and Paranormal Experience*, 1994.

Kastenbaum, Robert, and Beatrice Kastenbaum, eds. *Encyclopedia of Death*, 1993.

Melton, J. Gordon, ed. *New Age Almanac*, 1991.

*Mysteries of Mind, Space and Time: The Unexplained*. H. S. Stuttman, 1992.

*Parapsychology, New Age, and the Occult: A Source Encyclopedia*. Reference Press International, 1995.

## PERIODICAL INDEXES TO SEARCH (BOOKS OR CD-ROMS)

EBSCO Magazine Article Summaries

InfoTrac
NewsBank and other newspaper indexes
Readers' Guide to Periodical Literature
SIRS (Social Issues Resources Series)
WILSONDISC

## ONLINE DATABASES TO SEARCH

America Online
CompuServe
Dialog
Internet
Prodigy

## KEY WORDS AND DESCRIPTORS FOR PERIODICAL INDEX AND ONLINE SEARCHES

Near-death experiences
Deathbed hallucinations
Out-of-body experiences
Apparent death

## NATIONAL ORGANIZATION TO CONTACT FOR ADDITIONAL INFORMATION

International Association for Near-Death Studies, P.O. Box 7767, Philadelphia, PA 19101–7767.

## SUGGESTIONS FOR NARROWING THIS TOPIC

Describe some of the common experiences among near-death survivors.
Evaluate the role of religion in near-death experiences.
Investigate near-death-experience research as it pertains to children; to adults.

## SUGGESTIONS FOR RELATED TOPICS

Coma
Hypnotism
New Age movement
Reincarnation
Unconscious state

This RESEARCH TOPIC GUIDE is intended to help the library user find information and materials on a particular topic in many sources throughout the library. Resources on this topic are not limited to those described and availability will depend upon the individual library. Feel free to ask a librarian for assistance.

# New Age Movement

**BACKGROUND**

A controversial concept, the New Age movement does not fit neatly into a category. Believers have an interest in alternative philosophy and a desire to create a more humane and self-sufficient society. The New Age is often equated with psychic phenomena, spirituality, and the occult as well as holistic medicine, consciousness studies and environmental causes. New Age advocates attempt to integrate these diverse aspects of life into a harmonious and balanced whole.

**BROWSE FOR BOOKS ON THE SHELF USING THESE CALL NUMBERS**

> 016.78
> 131
> 133

**LOOK UNDER THE FOLLOWING SUBJECTS IN THE CATALOG (CARD OR COMPUTER)**

> New Age movement
> Spiritualism
> Parapsychology
> Use headings for specific New Age subjects.

**REFERENCE MATERIALS THAT MAY HELP (BOOKS OR CD-ROMS)**

> Birosik, Patti Jean. *The New Age Music Guide*, 1989.
> Gold, Gari. *The New Age A to Z (Xept X!): A Dictionary*, 1992.
> Melton, J. Gordon, et al. *New Age Almanac*, 1991.
> Rhodes, Ron. *New Age Movement: Zondervan Guide to Cults and Religious Movements*, 1995.

**PERIODICAL INDEXES TO SEARCH (BOOKS OR CD-ROMS)**

> EBSCO Magazine Article Summaries
> InfoTrac
> NewsBank and other newspaper indexes
> Readers' Guide to Periodical Literature
> SIRS (Social Issues Resources Series)
> WILSONDISC

**ONLINE DATABASES TO SEARCH**

> America Online
> CompuServe
> Dialog
> Internet
> Prodigy

## KEY WORDS AND DESCRIPTORS FOR PERIODICAL INDEX AND ONLINE SEARCHES

New Age movement
Self-help movement
Spirituality
Spiritualism
New Age music
Use key word for specific New Age subject; e.g., crystals, holistic medicine, New Age music.

## VIDEOTAPES ON THIS TOPIC

*Light of the Spirit*. Geffen Home Video, 1987.
*The New Believers: Inside the "New Age" Movement*. Monticello Productions, 1990.

## FICTION BOOKS RELATING TO TOPIC

Qualey, Marsha. *Everybody's Daughter*, 1991.
Tolan, Stephanie S. *A Good Courage*, 1988.

## NATIONAL ORGANIZATIONS TO CONTACT FOR ADDITIONAL INFORMATION

New Age World Religious and Scientific Research Foundation, 62091 Valley View Circle, Josua Tree, CA 92252.
Unarius Academy of Science, 145 S. Magnolia Ave., El Cahon, CA 92020–4522.

## SUGGESTIONS FOR NARROWING THIS TOPIC

Discuss Christianity and the New Age movement.
Evaluate the practice of dream interpretation.
Investigate healing through hypnotism.
Report on New Age retreats.
What is shamanism and how does it relate to New Age philosophy?

## SUGGESTIONS FOR RELATED TOPICS

Acupuncture
Astrology
Crystal energy
Holistic medicine
Macrobiotics
Reincarnation

This RESEARCH TOPIC GUIDE is intended to help the library user find information and materials on a particular topic in many sources throughout the library. Resources on this topic are not limited to those described and availability will depend upon the individual library. Feel free to ask a librarian for assistance.

# Police Brutality

**BACKGROUND**

The subject of police brutality has gained national prominence since the Rodney King case. Complaints of police brutality often come from minorities (blacks, Asians, gays, etc.) and community groups representing minorities.

**BROWSE FOR BOOKS ON THE SHELF USING THESE CALL NUMBERS**

> 363.2–363.232

**LOOK UNDER THE FOLLOWING SUBJECTS IN THE CATALOG (CARD OR COMPUTER)**

> Police—United States—Complaints against
> Discrimination in law enforcement—United States

**REFERENCE MATERIALS THAT MAY HELP (BOOKS OR CD-ROMS)**

> *CQ Researcher*, September 6, 1991; November 24, 1995.
> DiCanio, Margaret. *Encyclopedia of Violence*, 1993.
> *Editorials on File*. Facts on File.
> *Facts on File*
> General encyclopedias

**PERIODICAL INDEXES TO SEARCH (BOOKS OR CD-ROMS)**

> EBSCO Magazine Article Summaries
> InfoTrac
> NewsBank and other newspaper indexes
> Readers' Guide to Periodical Literature
> SIRS (Social Issues Resources Series)
> WILSONDISC

**ONLINE DATABASES TO SEARCH**

> America Online
> CompuServe
> Dialog
> Internet
> Prodigy

## KEY WORDS AND DESCRIPTORS FOR PERIODICAL INDEX AND ONLINE SEARCHES

Police brutality

Police—Complaints against

King, Rodney

## VIDEOTAPES ON THIS TOPIC

*Rodney King Case*. MPI Home Video, 1992.

*Street Cop*. PBS Video, 1987.

## NATIONAL ORGANIZATIONS TO CONTACT FOR ADDITIONAL INFORMATION

American Civil Liberties Union, 132 W. 33rd St., New York, NY 10036.

American Federation of Police, 3801 Biscayne Blvd., Miami, FL 33137.

## SUGGESTIONS FOR NARROWING THIS TOPIC

Discuss police conduct in minority communities.

How is police brutality portrayed in rap music?

Investigate the causes and/or solutions to the problem of police brutality.

Report on a particular case study of police brutality; e.g., Rodney King case.

## SUGGESTIONS FOR RELATED TOPICS

Los Angeles Police Department

Police corruption

Riots

Gangs

This RESEARCH TOPIC GUIDE is intended to help the library user find information and materials on a particular topic in many sources throughout the library. Resources on this topic are not limited to those described and availability will depend upon the individual library. Feel free to ask a librarian for assistance.

# Post-Traumatic Stress Disorder

## BACKGROUND

First documented in Vietnam veterans, post–traumatic stress disorder reveals itself in a variety of symptoms, including depression, substance abuse, emotional upset, suicidal tendencies, flashbacks, and an inability to get along in society. These symptoms can occur following exposure to extreme situations such as war, threat of death, disasters, and other violent conditions. Experts feel the fear and helpless horror experienced by the victims of post–traumatic stress disorder cause these symptoms.

## BROWSE FOR BOOKS ON THE SHELF USING THESE CALL NUMBERS

616.85–616.85212
355.1–355.1156

## LOOK UNDER THE FOLLOWING SUBJECTS IN THE CATALOG (CARD OR COMPUTER)

Post–traumatic stress disorder
Post–traumatic stress disorder—Case studies
Post–traumatic stress disorder—Treatment
Veterans—Mental health services—United States
Vietnamese Conflict, 1961–1975—Psychological aspects
War—Psychological aspects
Disasters—Psychological aspects

## REFERENCE MATERIALS THAT MAY HELP (BOOKS OR CD-ROMS)

American Psychological Association. *Diagnostic and Statistical Manual of Mental Disorders: DSM-IV*, 1994.

Hathaway, William E., et al. *Current Pediatric Diagnosis and Treatment*, 1994.

Rakel, Robert E., ed. *Conn's Current Therapy, 1995*, 1995.

Taylor, A.J.W. *Disasters and Disaster Stress*, 1989.

Tierney, Lawrence M., ed. *Current Medical Diagnosis and Treatment, 1995*, 1995.

Williams, Mary Beth. *Handbook of Post-Traumatic Therapy*, 1994.

## PERIODICAL INDEXES TO SEARCH (BOOKS OR CD-ROMS)

EBSCO Magazine Article Summaries
InfoTrac
NewsBank and other newspaper indexes
Readers' Guide to Periodical Literature

SIRS (Social Issues Resources Series)
WILSONDISC

## ONLINE DATABASES TO SEARCH

America Online
CompuServe
Dialog
Internet
Prodigy

## KEY WORDS AND DESCRIPTORS FOR PERIODICAL INDEX AND ONLINE SEARCHES

Post–traumatic stress disorder
Vietnamese Conflict, psychological aspects
Disasters—psychological aspects
Human behavior—post–traumatic stress disorder

## VIDEOTAPES ON THIS TOPIC

*Fearless*. Warner Home Video, 1993.
*The Nature of Stress*. Annenberg/CPB Collection, 1992.

## FICTION BOOKS RELATING TO TOPIC

Jensen, Kathryn. *Pocket Change*, 1989.
Wolkoff, Judie. *Where the Elf King Sings*, 1980.

## NATIONAL ORGANIZATION TO CONTACT FOR ADDITIONAL INFORMATION

International Society for Traumatic Stress Studies, 435 N. Michigan Ave., Ste. 1717, Chicago, IL 60611.

## SUGGESTIONS FOR NARROWING THIS TOPIC

Discuss the occurrence of post–traumatic stress disorder in one of the following groups of people: Vietnam veterans, urban teenagers, released hostages and prisoners of war, survivors of the Holocaust, victims of sexual assault, or airplane crash survivors.
Investigate the causes of post–traumatic stress disorder.

## SUGGESTIONS FOR RELATED TOPICS

Gulf War syndrome
Psychology of trauma
Rape trauma syndrome
Trauma in children

This RESEARCH TOPIC GUIDE is intended to help the library user find information and materials on a particular topic in many sources throughout the library. Resources on this topic are not limited to those described and availability will depend upon the individual library. Feel free to ask a librarian for assistance.

# Prison Reform

## BACKGROUND

The U.S. prison system deals with a multitude of problems, including overcrowding, inmate violence, riots, treatment of prisoners, high operating costs, and underpaid and undertrained personnel. Reformers attempt to find solutions to these issues and effectively implement them.

## BROWSE FOR BOOKS ON THE SHELF USING THESE CALL NUMBERS

365.7
365.973

## LOOK UNDER THE FOLLOWING SUBJECTS IN THE CATALOG (CARD OR COMPUTER)

Prisons
Prisons—United States
Prisons—United States—History
Corrections—United States
Rehabilitation of criminals—United States

## USE PAMPHLET FILE (ALSO CALLED VERTICAL FILE) UNDER THE HEADING

Prisons

## REFERENCE MATERIALS THAT MAY HELP (BOOKS OR CD-ROMS)

*CQ Researcher*, February 4, 1994.
*Editorials on File*, Facts on File.
*Facts on File*
General encyclopedias

## PERIODICAL INDEXES TO SEARCH (BOOKS OR CD-ROMS)

EBSCO Magazine Article Summaries
InfoTrac
NewsBank and other newspaper indexes
Readers' Guide to Periodical Literature
SIRS (Social Issues Resources Series)
WILSONDISC

## ONLINE DATABASES TO SEARCH

America Online
CompuServe
Dialog
Internet

## KEY WORDS AND DESCRIPTORS FOR PERIODICAL INDEX AND ONLINE SEARCHES

Prison overcrowding
Prison procedures
Prison reform
Prison reformers
Prison riots
Prisons—analysis
Prison security
Rehabilitation of criminals

## VIDEOTAPES ON THIS TOPIC

*Birdman of Alcatraz*. CBS/Fox Video, 1991.
*Murder in the First*. Warner Home Video, 1995.

## FICTION BOOKS RELATING TO TOPIC

Gaddis, Thomas E. *Birdman of Alcatraz*, 1955.
Gifaldi, David. *One Thing for Sure*, 1986.
Hyde, Dayton O. *Island of the Loons*, 1984.
Marsden, John. *Letters from the Inside*, 1994.

## NATIONAL ORGANIZATIONS TO CONTACT FOR ADDITIONAL INFORMATION

American Prison Association—American Correctional Association, 8025 Laurel Lakes Court, Laurel Lakes, MD 20707–5075.
National Prison Project, 1875 Connecticut Ave., N.W., Washington, DC 20009.

## SUGGESTIONS FOR NARROWING THIS TOPIC

Analyze a particular prison; e.g., Leavenworth, Attica.
Discuss the pros and cons of early release, furloughs, parole.
Discuss theories and practice of rehabilitation of prisoners.
Research one or more problems affecting prisons; e.g., overcrowding, riots, violence.

## SUGGESTIONS FOR RELATED TOPICS

Alternatives to imprisonment
Historic prisons; e.g., Alcatraz, Sing Sing
Notorious prison riots; e.g., Attica, Soledad
Prison reformers in history; e.g., Elizabeth Fry

This RESEARCH TOPIC GUIDE is intended to help the library user find information and materials on a particular topic in many sources throughout the library. Resources on this topic are not limited to those described and availability will depend upon the individual library. Feel free to ask a librarian for assistance.

# Privatization of Schools

## BACKGROUND

In the wake of declining SAT scores, the public sense that there is a decline in the quality of education, and the general agreement that schools need to be improved, privatization of schools is under consideration by many districts. Privatization, the provision of public services by the private sector, is being debated by educators in communities across the country as a possible solution. Some school systems are now managed by private companies while others contract out certain educational services.

## BROWSE FOR BOOKS ON THE SHELF USING THESE CALL NUMBERS

338.973

371–371.01

379.13

## LOOK UNDER THE FOLLOWING SUBJECTS IN THE CATALOG (CARD OR COMPUTER)

School choice—United States

Privatization—United States

Education—United States—Aims and objectives

## REFERENCE MATERIALS THAT MAY HELP (BOOKS OR CD-ROMS)

*CQ Researcher*, March 25, 1994.

*Editorials on File*, Facts on File.

*Facts on File*

Mintz, Jerry, ed. *Handbook of Alternative Education*, 1994.

## PERIODICAL INDEXES TO SEARCH (BOOKS OR CD-ROMS)

EBSCO Magazine Article Summaries

InfoTrac

NewsBank and other newspaper indexes

Readers' Guide to Periodical Literature

SIRS (Social Issues Resources Series)

WILSONDISC

## ONLINE DATABASES TO SEARCH

Dialog

Internet

## KEY WORDS AND DESCRIPTORS FOR PERIODICAL INDEX AND ONLINE SEARCHES

Public schools—privatization

Public schools—contracts and services

School choice—United States

School privatization

Public school administration—reorganization

## NATIONAL ORGANIZATIONS TO CONTACT FOR ADDITIONAL INFORMATION

Educational Alternatives, Inc., 1300 Norwest Financial Center, 7900 Xerxes Ave. South, Minneapolis, MN 55431.

National Education Association, 1201 16th St., N.W., Washington, DC 20036.

Whittle Communications Ltd. Partnership, 333 W. Main St., Knoxville, TN 37902.

## SUGGESTIONS FOR NARROWING THIS TOPIC

Present the case for (or against) the privatization of schools.

Research a school system that has opted for privatization; e.g., Baltimore, Hartford, Miami, Minneapolis.

## SUGGESTIONS FOR RELATED TOPICS

School choice

School reform

Voucher plan

Whittle Corporation

This RESEARCH TOPIC GUIDE is intended to help the library user find information and materials on a particular topic in many sources throughout the library. Resources on this topic are not limited to those described and availability will depend upon the individual library. Feel free to ask a librarian for assistance.

# Psychological Aspects of Advertising

**BACKGROUND**

Use of subliminal advertising techniques by the advertising industry to help sell products is a much-debated topic. Some researchers have determined that people can detect subtle signals to the subconscious. But has the practice proved effective and is it ethical?

**BROWSE FOR BOOKS ON THE SHELF USING THESE CALL NUMBERS**

> 658.1019
> 658.85
> 659.1–659.1042
> 303.375
> 301.154

**LOOK UNDER THE FOLLOWING SUBJECTS IN THE CATALOG (CARD OR COMPUTER)**

> Advertising—Psychological aspects
> Advertising—United States
> Selling—Psychological aspects
> Subliminal projection
> Persuasion (Psychology)
> Consumer behavior

**REFERENCE MATERIALS THAT MAY HELP (BOOKS OR CD-ROMS)**

> Corsini, Raymond J. *Encyclopedia of Psychology*, 1994.
> *Editorials on File*, Facts on File.

**PERIODICAL INDEXES TO SEARCH (BOOKS OR CD-ROMS)**

> EBSCO Magazine Article Summaries
> InfoTrac
> NewsBank and other newspaper indexes
> Readers' Guide to Periodical Literature
> SIRS (Social Issues Resources Series)
> WILSONDISC

**ONLINE DATABASES TO SEARCH**

> Dialog
> Internet

## KEY WORDS AND DESCRIPTORS FOR PERIODICAL INDEX AND ONLINE SEARCHES

Subliminal perception
Subliminal projection
Advertising ethics
Advertising—Psychological aspects

## VIDEOTAPES ON THIS TOPIC

*Beneath the Surface*. Intelecom, 1992.
*The 30-Second Seduction*. Films, Inc., 1985.

## NATIONAL ORGANIZATION TO CONTACT FOR ADDITIONAL INFORMATION

Advertising Research Foundation, 3 E. 54th St., New York, NY 10022.

## SUGGESTIONS FOR NARROWING THIS TOPIC

Choose a specific advertising campaign and analyze use of subliminal advertising.
Discuss possible harmful effects of subliminal advertising.
What is subliminal advertising and how does it work?

## SUGGESTIONS FOR RELATED TOPICS

Brainwashing
Marketing
Propaganda
Subliminal learning
Television advertising and children

This RESEARCH TOPIC GUIDE is intended to help the library user find information and materials on a particular topic in many sources throughout the library. Resources on this topic are not limited to those described and availability will depend upon the individual library. Feel free to ask a librarian for assistance.

# Rock Music Lyrics—Moral and Ethical Aspects

## BACKGROUND

Can music lyrics incite people to harm themselves, commit suicide, or cause violence to others? Should pornographic lyrics be against the law? These are some of the issues at the center of the ongoing controversy over rap, rock, and heavy metal music lyrics.

## BROWSE FOR BOOKS ON THE SHELF USING THESE CALL NUMBERS

781.63–781.96
782.4216
784.54–784.55
302.23
323.445

## LOOK UNDER THE FOLLOWING SUBJECTS IN THE CATALOG (CARD OR COMPUTER)

Heavy metal (Music)—History and criticism
Rap (Music)—History and criticism
Rap (Music)—Texts
Rock music—History and criticism
Rock music—Texts
Rock music—Themes, motives, Literary
Rock music—United States—History and criticism
Censorship

## REFERENCE MATERIALS THAT MAY HELP (BOOKS OR CD-ROMS)

*CQ Researcher*, December 20, 1991.
Draper, James P., ed. *Contemporary Literary Criticism*, Vol. 76, 1993.
*Facts on File*
Macken, Bob. *The Rock Music Source Book*, 1980.
McCoy, Judy. *Rap Music in the 1980s: A Reference Guide*, 1992.

## PERIODICAL INDEXES TO SEARCH (BOOKS OR CD-ROMS)

EBSCO Magazine Article Summaries
InfoTrac
NewsBank and other newspaper indexes
Readers' Guide to Periodical Literature
SIRS (Social Issues Resources Series)
WILSONDISC

## ONLINE DATABASES TO SEARCH

America Online
CompuServe

Dialog
Internet
Prodigy

## KEY WORDS AND DESCRIPTORS FOR PERIODICAL INDEX AND ONLINE SEARCHES

Heavy metal music—moral and religious aspects
Rap music—moral and religious aspects
Rock music—moral and religious aspects
Lyrics—moral and ethical aspects
Police brutality in rap music
Race relations in rap music
Sound recordings—censorship
Phonograph records—labeling
Obscenity

## VIDEOTAPE ON THIS TOPIC

*Damned in the USA*. Gabriel Films, 1992.

## FICTION BOOKS RELATING TO TOPIC

Block, Francesca Lia. *Cherokee Bat and the Goat Guys*, 1992.
Cooney, Caroline. *Don't Blame the Music*, 1986.

## NATIONAL ORGANIZATIONS TO CONTACT FOR ADDITIONAL INFORMATION

American Civil Liberties Union, 132 W. 43rd St., New York, NY 10036.
Parents Music Resource Center, 1500 Arlington Blvd., Arlington, VA 22209.
Rock and Roll Society International Political Action Committee, P.O. Box 1949, New Haven, CT 06510.

## SUGGESTIONS FOR NARROWING THIS TOPIC

Discuss the constitutionality of censoring music lyrics.
Evaluate the effect of rap (rock, etc.) music on behavior.
Investigate the effects of rap lyrics on black youth.
Report on a specific performer or group in terms of lyrics; e.g., 2 Live Crew, Ice-T, Sister Souljah.

## SUGGESTIONS FOR RELATED TOPICS

Hate crimes
Lyrics of Beatles songs (or any other group)
Popular culture vs. traditional values
Rap music and black culture

This RESEARCH TOPIC GUIDE is intended to help the library user find information and materials on a particular topic in many sources throughout the library. Resources on this topic are not limited to those described and availability will depend upon the individual library. Feel free to ask a librarian for assistance.

# Sexual Harassment

## BACKGROUND

Sexual harassment has been exposed to increasing public scrutiny and discussion in recent years. The Equal Employment Opportunity Commission (EEOC) defines sexual harassment as unwelcome sexual advances, requests for sexual favors, and other verbal or physical conduct of a sexual nature. Both women and men can be the perpetrators or victims of this damaging social problem.

## BROWSE FOR BOOKS ON THE SHELF USING THESE CALL NUMBERS

> 331.4133
> 305.3
> 305.42
> 306.7

## LOOK UNDER THE FOLLOWING SUBJECTS IN THE CATALOG (CARD OR COMPUTER)

> Sexual harassment
> Sexual harassment of women
> Sexual harassment of women—United States
> Sex in the workplace
> Sex role in the work environment

## USE PAMPHLET FILE (ALSO CALLED VERTICAL FILE) UNDER THE HEADINGS

> Sex discrimination
> Sexual harassment

## REFERENCE MATERIALS THAT MAY HELP (BOOKS OR CD-ROMS)

> *CQ Researcher*, August 9, 1991.
> *Facts on File*
> Trager, Oliver, ed. *Sexual Politics in America*, 1994.
> Westheimer, Ruth K. *Dr. Ruth's Encyclopedia of Sex*, 1994.

## PERIODICAL INDEXES TO SEARCH (BOOKS OR CD-ROMS)

> EBSCO Magazine Article Summaries
> InfoTrac
> NewsBank and other newspaper indexes
> Readers' Guide to Periodical Literature
> SIRS (Social Issues Resources Series)
> WILSONDISC

## ONLINE DATABASES TO SEARCH

> America Online
> CompuServe

Dialog
Internet
Prodigy

## KEY WORDS AND DESCRIPTORS FOR PERIODICAL INDEX AND ONLINE SEARCHES

Sexual harassment
Sex in business
Women in the workforce
Discrimination in employment—sexual harassment
Work environment—moral and ethical aspects

## VIDEOTAPES ON THIS TOPIC

*Dealing with Sexual Harassment in the Work Place.* American Business Videos, 1992.
*Sexual Harassment Crossing the Line.* Cambridge Educational, 11993.
*Sexual Harassment from 9 to 5.* Films for the Humanities, 1986.

## FICTION BOOKS RELATING TO TOPIC

Conford, Ellen. *To All My Fans, with Love, from Sylvie*, 1983.
Mazer, Norma Fox. *Out of Control*, 1993.
Pfeffer, Susan Beth. *The Ring of Truth*, 1993.

## NATIONAL ORGANIZATIONS TO CONTACT FOR ADDITIONAL INFORMATION

Association for the Sexually Harassed, P.O. Box 27235, Philadelphia, PA 19118.
9 to 5, National Association of Working Women, 614 Superior Ave., N.W., Rm. 852, Cleveland, OH 44113.

## SUGGESTIONS FOR NARROWING THIS TOPIC

Discuss sexual harassment in the office, military, or colleges and universities.
Investigate the legal aspects of sexual harassment.
Report on a nationally prominent case of sexual harassment; e.g., Robert Packwood, Clarence Thomas, Benjamin Chavis.

## SUGGESTIONS FOR RELATED TOPICS

Hate crimes
Sex crimes
Sex discrimination against women and men
Sex roles in the workplace
Stalking

This RESEARCH TOPIC GUIDE is intended to help the library user find information and materials on a particular topic in many sources throughout the library. Resources on this topic are not limited to those described and availability will depend upon the individual library. Feel free to ask a librarian for assistance.

# Single-Sex Schools

## BACKGROUND

The topic of single-sex schools has become a controversial issue in education. Coeducational programs are consistent with the spirit of democracy and equal opportunity supported by the United States; however, as recent studies have indicated, women may be short-changed in traditional classrooms and do better academically and emotionally in a single-sex environment. Other research done with African-American boys in urban elementary schools suggests that they, too, develop higher levels of self-esteem in a single-gender situation.

## BROWSE FOR BOOKS ON THE SHELF USING THESE CALL NUMBERS

370.1934

376.65

## LOOK UNDER THE FOLLOWING SUBJECTS IN THE CATALOG (CARD OR COMPUTER)

Sex differences in education

Sex discrimination in education—United States

Sexism in education—United States

Women—Education—United States

## REFERENCE MATERIALS THAT MAY HELP (BOOKS OR CD-ROMS)

*Congressional Quarterly*, August 6, 1994.

*CQ Researcher*, June 3, 1994.

Stitt, Beverly A. *Gender Equity in Education: An Annotated Bibliography*, 1994.

## PERIODICAL INDEXES TO SEARCH (BOOKS OR CD-ROMS)

EBSCO Magazine Article Summaries

InfoTrac

NewsBank and other newspaper indexes

Readers' Guide to Periodical Literature

SIRS (Social Issues Resources Series)

WILSONDISC

## ONLINE DATABASES TO SEARCH

America Online

CompuServe

Dialog

Internet

Prodigy

## KEY WORDS AND DESCRIPTORS FOR PERIODICAL INDEX AND ONLINE SEARCHES

Single-sex schools

Women's colleges

Coeducation

Colleges for women

Education and learning—studies and reports—gender bias

Gender bias

Sex discrimination in education

## NATIONAL ORGANIZATIONS TO CONTACT FOR ADDITIONAL INFORMATION

AAUW (American Association of University Women) Educational Foundation, 111 16th St., N.W., Washington, DC 20036.

Center for Women Policy Studies, 2000 P St., N.W., Ste. 508, Washington, DC 20036.

## SUGGESTIONS FOR NARROWING THIS TOPIC

Do girls develop more self-esteem in a single-sex setting?

Investigate whether or not females are shortchanged in co-ed education.

Research the topic of single-sex schools and inner-city youth.

## SUGGESTIONS FOR RELATED TOPICS

Integration, by females, of military schools; e.g., the Citadel, West Point

Women's studies curricula

Sexism in textbooks

Teacher bias toward males in the classroom

This RESEARCH TOPIC GUIDE is intended to help the library user find information and materials on a particular topic in many sources throughout the library. Resources on this topic are not limited to those described and availability will depend upon the individual library. Feel free to ask a librarian for assistance.

# Teenage Pregnancy

**BACKGROUND**

Although exposed to birth control information and sex education, teenagers continue to become pregnant. The reasons for this phenomenon are debated while programs to prevent teenage pregnancy are promoted in schools and communities nationwide.

**BROWSE FOR BOOKS ON THE SHELF USING THESE CALL NUMBERS**

>306.7–306.856
>362.8284–362.8392

**LOOK UNDER THE FOLLOWING SUBJECTS IN THE CATALOG (CARD OR COMPUTER)**

>Teenage pregnancy—United States
>Teenage mothers—United States
>Teenage parents—United States
>Unmarried mothers

**USE PAMPHLET FILE (ALSO CALLED VERTICAL FILE) UNDER THE HEADING**

>Teenage pregnancy

**REFERENCE MATERIALS THAT MAY HELP (BOOKS OR CD-ROMS)**

>*CQ Researcher*, May 14, 1993; July 5, 1991.
>DeCherney, Alan H., and Martin L. Pernoll, eds. *Current Obstetric and Gynecologic Diagnosis and Treatment*, 1994.
>Hempelman, Kathleen A. *Teen Legal Rights: A Guide for the '90s*, 1994.
>Westheimer, Ruth K. *Dr. Ruth's Encyclopedia of Sex*, 1994.

**PERIODICAL INDEXES TO SEARCH (BOOKS OR CD-ROMS)**

>EBSCO Magazine Article Summaries
>InfoTrac
>NewsBank and other newspaper indexes
>Readers' Guide to Periodical Literature
>SIRS (Social Issues Resources Series)
>WILSONDISC

**ONLINE DATABASES TO SEARCH**

>America Online
>CompuServe
>Dialog
>Internet
>Prodigy

## KEY WORDS AND DESCRIPTORS FOR PERIODICAL INDEX AND ONLINE SEARCHES

Teenage pregnancy
Teenage mothers
Pregnancy—teenagers
Pregnant schoolgirls
Unwed mothers

## VIDEOTAPES ON THIS TOPIC

*Teenage Pregnancy*. Films for the Humanities and Sciences, 1990.
*Teenage Pregnancy and Prevention*. Human Relations Media, 1986.

## FICTION BOOKS RELATING TO TOPIC

Doherty, Berlie. *Dear Nobody*, 1992.
Johnson, Lissa Hall. *Just like Ice Cream*, 1995.
Myers, Walter Dean. *Sweet Illusions*, 1986.
Woodson, Jacqueline. *The Dear One*, 1993.

## NATIONAL ORGANIZATIONS TO CONTACT FOR ADDITIONAL INFORMATION

Planned Parenthood Federation of America, 810 7th Ave., New York, NY 10019.
SIECUS (Sex Information and Education Council of the United States), 130 W. 42nd St., Ste. 2500, New York, NY 10036.

## SUGGESTIONS FOR NARROWING THIS TOPIC

Discuss the moral and ethical aspects of teenage pregnancy.
Evaluate the impact of teenage pregnancy on society.
Investigate the availability of prenatal care for pregnant teenagers.
Research the causes of teenage pregnancy.

## SUGGESTIONS FOR RELATED TOPICS

Abortion
Adoption
Fetal alcohol syndrome
Sex education
Teenage sexuality

This RESEARCH TOPIC GUIDE is intended to help the library user find information and materials on a particular topic in many sources throughout the library. Resources on this topic are not limited to those described and availability will depend upon the individual library. Feel free to ask a librarian for assistance.

# Teenage Suicide

## BACKGROUND

Teenagers choose suicide for many reasons, including depression, drug abuse, family problems, low self-esteem, suicide pacts, or combinations of these and other problems. Professionals and peer counselors who work with adolescents research the topic of teenage suicide in an attempt to understand the causes and to seek solutions to this tragedy.

## BROWSE FOR BOOKS ON THE SHELF USING THESE CALL NUMBERS

362.2–362.28
616.85–616.8584
179.7

## LOOK UNDER THE FOLLOWING SUBJECTS IN THE CATALOG (CARD OR COMPUTER)

Suicide
Suicide—In adolescence
Youth—Suicidal behavior

## REFERENCE MATERIALS THAT MAY HELP (BOOKS OR CD-ROMS)

Corsini, Raymond J. *Encyclopedia of Psychology*, 1994.
*CQ Researcher*, June 14, 1991.
Evans, Glen, and Norman L. Farberow. *The Encyclopedia of Suicide*, 1988. *Facts on File*
Kastenbaum, Robert, and Beatrice Kastenbaum, eds. *The Encyclopedia of Death*, 1993.

## PERIODICAL INDEXES TO SEARCH (BOOKS OR CD-ROMS)

EBSCO Magazine Article Summaries
InfoTrac
NewsBank and other newspaper indexes
Readers' Guide to Periodical Literature
SIRS (Social Issues Resources Series)
WILSONDISC

## ONLINE DATABASES TO SEARCH

America Online
CompuServe
Dialog

Internet
Prodigy

## KEY WORDS AND DESCRIPTORS FOR PERIODICAL INDEX AND ONLINE SEARCHES

Suicide
Teenage suicide
Teenage suicide prevention
Teenagers—psychology and mental health

## VIDEOTAPES ON THIS TOPIC

*Teenage Depression and Suicide*. Schlessinger Video Productions, 1991.
*Teenage Suicide*. NPI Video, 1987.
*Teen Suicides, Why?* PBS Video, 1991.

## FICTION BOOKS RELATING TO TOPIC

Crutcher, Chris. *Chinese Handcuffs*, 1989.
Lemieux, A.C. *The TV Guidance Counselor*, 1993.
Dragonwagon, Crescent. *The Year It Rained*, 1985.

## NATIONAL ORGANIZATIONS TO CONTACT FOR ADDITIONAL INFORMATION

Youth Suicide Prevention, 11 Parkman Way, Needham, MA 02192-2863.
Youth Suicide National Center, 445 Virginia Ave., San Mateo, CA 94402.

## SUGGESTIONS FOR NARROWING THIS TOPIC

Analyze some of the causes of suicidal behavior among teenagers.
Discuss the moral and ethical aspects of teenage suicide.
How do suicide hotlines operate?
Investigate the legal aspects of suicide.

## SUGGESTIONS FOR RELATED TOPICS

Adolescent psychology
Depression in teenagers
Rock music lyrics
Right to die

This RESEARCH TOPIC GUIDE is intended to help the library user find information and materials on a particular topic in many sources throughout the library. Resources on this topic are not limited to those described and availability will depend upon the individual library. Feel free to ask a librarian for assistance.

# Television and Its Effects on Youth

**BACKGROUND**

Does watching violence on television cause aggressiveness or criminal behavior among youth? Does sexually explicit programming negatively affect impressionable teens? Studies by social psychologists, consumer groups, and the broadcasting industry have produced often conflicting results. Although most groups agree that behavior is affected by television, exactly how it is affected is debated.

**BROWSE FOR BOOKS ON THE SHELF USING THESE CALL NUMBERS**

301.16
302.2345
343.73
384.55

**LOOK UNDER THE FOLLOWING SUBJECTS IN THE CATALOG (CARD OR COMPUTER)**

Television and children
Violence in television
Television programs
Television—Law and legislation—United States
Television and family
Television broadcasting—Social aspects—United States

**REFERENCE MATERIALS THAT MAY HELP (BOOKS OR CD-ROMS)**

*CQ Researcher*, March 26, 1993; November 17, 1995.
*Editorials on File*, Facts on File.
*Facts on File*

**PERIODICAL INDEXES TO SEARCH (BOOKS OR CD-ROMS)**

EBSCO Magazine Article Summaries
InfoTrac
NewsBank and other newspaper indexes
Readers' Guide to Periodical Literature
SIRS (Social Issues Resources Series)
WILSONDISC

**ONLINE DATABASES TO SEARCH**

America Online
CompuServe

Dialog

Internet

Prodigy

## KEY WORDS AND DESCRIPTORS FOR PERIODICAL INDEX AND ONLINE SEARCHES

Television and youth

Television and children

Sex in television

Violence in television

Television—influence

Television programs for children—psychological aspects

## VIDEOTAPE ON THIS TOPIC

*On Television: The Violence Factor.* Films, Inc., 1989.

## NATIONAL ORGANIZATIONS TO CONTACT FOR ADDITIONAL INFORMATION

Council for Children's Television and Media, 33290 W. 14 Mile Rd., Ste. 488, West Bloomfield, MI 48322.

National Coalition on Television Violence, P.O. Box 2157, Champaign, IL 61825.

## SUGGESTIONS FOR NARROWING THIS TOPIC

Comment on television as a positive influence.

Discuss the psychological impact of MTV on teenagers.

Evaluate research on television viewing and aggressiveness in children.

Is there a connection between television viewing and literacy?

Report on a particular television program and its possible effects on young viewers.

## SUGGESTIONS FOR RELATED TOPICS

Broadcasting and the First Amendment to the Constitution

Public television

Television advertising

Television in the classroom

This RESEARCH TOPIC GUIDE is intended to help the library user find information and materials on a particular topic in many sources throughout the library. Resources on this topic are not limited to those described and availability will depend upon the individual library. Feel free to ask a librarian for assistance.

# Terrorism

## BACKGROUND

Terrorism has occurred in various forms for hundreds of years but has been increasing in scope and intensity in the last several decades. Politically motivated, terrorism involves planned acts of brutality and violence committed by one or more people against governments, religious groups, and citizens. Because terrorism has become such a devastating world problem, governments and experts in the field are searching for solutions.

## BROWSE FOR BOOKS ON THE SHELF USING THESE CALL NUMBERS

303.62–303.625
301.633
363.32
364.1–364.154

## LOOK UNDER THE FOLLOWING SUBJECTS IN THE CATALOG (CARD OR COMPUTER)

Terrorism
Terrorists

## REFERENCE MATERIALS THAT MAY HELP (BOOKS OR CD-ROMS)

Anderson, Sean, ed. *The Historical Dictionary of Terrorism*, 1995.

Atkins, Stephen E. *Terrorism: A Reference Handbook*, 1992.

Magill, Frank N., ed. *Great Events from History II: Human Rights Series*, 1992.

Shafritz, Jay M., et al. *Almanac of Modern Terrorism*, 1991.

*Yearbook of the United Nations*, 1994.

General encyclopedias

## PERIODICAL INDEXES TO SEARCH (BOOKS OR CD-ROMS)

EBSCO Magazine Article Summaries
InfoTrac
NewsBank and other national newspaper indexes
Readers' Guide to Periodical Literature
SIRS (Social Issues Resources Series)
WILSONDISC

## ONLINE DATABASES TO SEARCH

American Online
CompuServe

Dialog
Internet
Prodigy

## KEY WORDS AND DESCRIPTORS FOR PERIODICAL INDEX AND ONLINE SEARCHES

Terrorism
Terrorists
Bombings
Bombs and bombings
Assassination
Hostage taking
Hostages

## VIDEOTAPES ON THIS TOPIC

*In the Name of the Father*. MCA Universal Home Video, 1994.
*Terrorism, the New World War*. MPI Home Video, 1989.

## FICTION BOOKS RELATING TO TOPIC

Cormier, Robert. *After the First Death*, 1979.
Johnson, Norma. *The Delphic Choice,* 1989.
Townsend, Tom. *Trader Wooly and the Terrorist*, 1988.

## SUGGESTIONS FOR NARROWING THIS TOPIC

Analyze the depiction of terrorism in motion pictures or television.
Discuss the political aspects of terrorism.
Investigate the various forms of terrorism; e.g., hijacking, hostage taking.
Report on a specific terrorist incident; e.g., Pan Am Flight 103, World Trade Center bombing.
Research the historical origins of terrorism in a particular region.

## SUGGESTIONS FOR RELATED TOPICS

Counterterrorism efforts
Genocide
Hate crimes
Mothers of the Plaza
Paramilitary groups
Saddam Hussein

This RESEARCH TOPIC GUIDE is intended to help the library user find information and materials on a particular topic in many sources throughout the library. Resources on this topic are not limited to those described and availability will depend upon the individual library. Feel free to ask a librarian for assistance.

# Tobacco Industry

## BACKGROUND

Although the United States has become increasingly aware of the dangers posed by the use of tobacco products, people continue to smoke, including large numbers of youth. Despite their strong lobbying efforts, the tobacco industry has come under fire by citizens groups and Congress. Regardless, tobacco companies continue manufacturing their products and marketing them at home and abroad.

## BROWSE FOR BOOKS ON THE SHELF USING THESE CALL NUMBERS

    338.4–338.47679
    331.7
    362.296
    363.19
    381.456797

## LOOK UNDER THE FOLLOWING SUBJECTS IN THE CATALOG (CARD OR COMPUTER)

    Tobacco industry
    Tobacco industry—Government policy
    Tobacco industry—United States
    Tobacco industry—United States—History

## USE PAMPHLET FILE (ALSO CALLED VERTICAL FILE) UNDER THE HEADINGS

    Drugs and drug abuse
    Smoking

## REFERENCE MATERIALS THAT MAY HELP (BOOKS OR CD-ROMS)

    *Congressional Quarterly Weekly Report*
    *CQ Researcher*, September 13, 1991; December 4, 1992; and September 30, 1994.
    *Editorials on File*, Facts on File.
    *Facts on File*
    Jaffe, Jerome H., ed. *Encyclopedia of Drugs and Alcohol*, 1994.

## PERIODICAL INDEXES TO SEARCH (BOOKS OR CD-ROMS)

    EBSCO Magazine Article Summaries
    InfoTrac
    NewsBank and other newspaper indexes
    Readers' Guide to Periodical Literature
    SIRS (Social Issues Resources Series)
    WILSONDISC

## ONLINE DATABASES TO SEARCH

    America Online
    CompuServe
    Dialog

Internet
Prodigy

## KEY WORDS AND DESCRIPTORS FOR PERIODICAL INDEX AND ONLINE SEARCHES

Tobacco industry
Tobacco
Cigarette industry
Smoking and tobacco
Farming and agribusiness—tobacco

## VIDEOTAPES ON THIS TOPIC

*Cigarettes: Who Profits? Who Dies?* Films for the Humanities and Sciences, 1992.
*Tobacco on Trial.* PBS Video, 1986.
*Tobacco Wars.* Yorkshire Television, 1992.

## FICTION BOOKS RELATING TO TOPIC

Buckley, Christopher. *Thank You for Smoking,* 1994. (adult)
Ellis, Julie. *Lasting Treasures,* 1993. (adult)
McLaurin, Tim. *Cured by Fire,* 1995. (adult)

## NATIONAL ORGANIZATIONS TO CONTACT FOR ADDITIONAL INFORMATION

Coalition on Smoking or Health, 1150 Connecticut Ave., N.W., Ste. 820, Washington, DC 20036.
Museum of Tobacco Art and History, 800 Harrison St., Nashville, TN 37203.
Tobacco Institute, 1875 Eye St., N.W., Ste. 800, Washington, DC 20006.

## SUGGESTIONS FOR NARROWING THIS TOPIC

Comment on the moral and ethical aspects of cigarette advertising.
Discuss the economic impact of the tobacco industry on a tobacco-growing state; e.g., Virginia, North Carolina.
Examine the influence and importance of the tobacco industry lobby.
Present the case for (or against) a ban on cigarette vending machines.
Report on a specific tobacco company; e.g., R. J. Reynolds, Philip Morris.
Research the history of the tobacco industry in the United States.

## SUGGESTIONS FOR RELATED TOPICS

Smoking—health aspects
Drug abuse
Liquor industry

This RESEARCH TOPIC GUIDE is intended to help the library user find information and materials on a particular topic in many sources throughout the library. Resources on this topic are not limited to those described and availability will depend upon the individual library. Feel free to ask a librarian for assistance.

# Vegetarianism

## BACKGROUND

The ranks of vegetarians are growing as more doctors and nutritionists recognize and promote the health benefits of consuming less meat and more vegetables, fruits, and grains. In addition, some are turning to a vegetarian lifestyle to protest the needless slaughter of animals.

## BROWSE FOR BOOKS ON THE SHELF USING THESE CALL NUMBERS

613.26–613.262
641.563–641.5636
179.3

## LOOK UNDER THE FOLLOWING SUBJECTS IN THE CATALOG (CARD OR COMPUTER)

Vegetarianism
Vegetarianism—Social aspects
Vegetarian children
Vegetarian cookery

## USE PAMPHLET FILE (ALSO CALLED VERTICAL FILE) UNDER THE HEADING

Vegetarianism

## REFERENCE MATERIALS THAT MAY HELP (BOOKS OR CD-ROMS)

*CQ Researcher*, May 24, 1991.

Herbert, Victor, and Gennell J. Subak-Sharpe, eds. *The Mount Sinai School of Medicine Complete Book of Nutrition*, 1990.

Nelson, Jennifer K., et al., eds. *Mayo Clinic Diet Manual: A Handbook of Nutrition Practices*, 1994.

## PERIODICAL INDEXES TO SEARCH (BOOKS OR CD-ROMS)

EBSCO Magazine Article Summaries
InfoTrac
NewsBank and other newspaper indexes
Readers' Guide to Periodical Literature
SIRS (Social Issues Resources Series)
WILSONDISC

## ONLINE DATABASES TO SEARCH

America Online
CompuServe
Dialog
Internet
Prodigy

## KEY WORDS AND DESCRIPTORS FOR PERIODICAL INDEX AND ONLINE SEARCHES

Vegetarianism
Vegetarians
Vegans

## FICTION BOOK RELATING TO TOPIC

Keller, Beverly. *Fowl Play, Desdemona*, 1989.

## NATIONAL ORGANIZATIONS TO CONTACT FOR ADDITIONAL INFORMATION

North American Vegetarian Society, P.O. Box 72, Dolgeville, NY 13329.
Vegetarian Resource Group, P.O. Box 1463, Baltimore, MD 21203.

## SUGGESTIONS FOR NARROWING THIS TOPIC

Discuss the political aspects of vegetarianism.
Evaluate the nutritional aspects of a vegetarian diet.
Investigate vegetarian cookery and recipes.
Research the special needs of teenage vegetarians.
Report on the topic of vegetarian restaurants.

## SUGGESTIONS FOR RELATED TOPICS

Animal rights
Natural foods
Medicinal plants
Macrobiotic diet
Reducing diets

This RESEARCH TOPIC GUIDE is intended to help the library user find information and materials on a particular topic in many sources throughout the library. Resources on this topic are not limited to those described and availability will depend upon the individual library. Feel free to ask a librarian for assistance.

# Violence in the Schools

## BACKGROUND

Schools in the United States, city, rural, and suburban, are struggling with a chronic problem of violence in and outside the classroom. The disruption is no longer confined to fist fights at recess and after-school bullying. Today students are armed with guns and using them to settle arguments and enhance reputation.

## BROWSE FOR BOOKS ON THE SHELF USING THESE CALL NUMBERS

363.33
364.36
303.6

## LOOK UNDER THE FOLLOWING SUBJECTS IN THE CATALOG (CARD OR COMPUTER)

School violence—United States
Juvenile delinquency—United States
Gangs
Gangs—United States
Violent crimes—United States
Violence

## REFERENCE MATERIALS THAT MAY HELP (BOOKS OR CD-ROMS)

*CQ Researcher*, September 11, 1992.
DiCanio, Margaret. *Encyclopedia of Violence*, 1993.
*Editorials on File*, Facts on File.
*Facts on File*

## PERIODICAL INDEXES TO SEARCH (BOOKS OR CD-ROMS)

EBSCO Magazine Article Summaries
InfoTrac
NewsBank and other newspaper indexes
Readers' Guide to Periodical Literature
SIRS (Social Issues Resources Series)
WILSONDISC

## ONLINE DATABASES TO SEARCH

America Online
CompuServe

Dialog
Internet
Prodigy

## KEY WORDS AND DESCRIPTORS FOR PERIODICAL INDEX AND ONLINE SEARCHES

School violence
Youth and firearms
Gangs
High schools—security measures
Public schools—crime

## VIDEOTAPE ON THIS TOPIC

*Real Men Don't Bleed*. MTI Film and Video, 1991.

## FICTION BOOKS RELATING TO TOPIC

Baer, Judy. *Double Danger*, 1994.
Hinton, S. E. *That Was Then, This Is Now*, 1971.
Shafer, J. *Smile or Die!*, 1994

## NATIONAL ORGANIZATION TO CONTACT FOR ADDITIONAL INFORMATION

National Education Association, 1201 16th St., N.W., Washington, DC 20036.

## SUGGESTIONS FOR NARROWING THIS TOPIC

Analyze the connection between drugs and violence in schools.
Evaluate different security measures effected by schools; e.g., metal detectors.
Discuss causes and/or solutions to the problem of violence in schools.
Investigate gang-related violence in schools.

## SUGGESTIONS FOR RELATED TOPICS

Dress codes
Gun control
Peer mediation programs
Violence in sports

This RESEARCH TOPIC GUIDE is intended to help the library user find information and materials on a particular topic in many sources throughout the library. Resources on this topic are not limited to those described and availability will depend upon the individual library. Feel free to ask a librarian for assistance.

# Welfare Reform

## BACKGROUND

The national debate over welfare reform continues to spiral. Most agree that the costs, both social and financial, are unacceptable and that the system is failing to help many of those for which it was originally intended. Disagreement involves whether to eliminate welfare or reform it, and if so, how.

## BROWSE FOR BOOKS ON THE SHELF USING THESE CALL NUMBERS

361.6–361.62
361.973
362.50973–362.58
323.042

## LOOK UNDER THE FOLLOWING SUBJECTS IN THE CATALOG (CARD OR COMPUTER)

Public welfare—United States
Public welfare
United States—Social policy—1980–
Economic assistance, Domestic—United States
Poor—United States
Poverty

## REFERENCE MATERIALS THAT MAY HELP (BOOKS OR CD-ROMS)

*Congressional Quarterly Weekly Report*
*CQ Researcher*, April 10, 1992; September 16, 1994.
*Editorials on File*, Facts on File.
*Facts on File*
General encyclopedias

## PERIODICAL INDEXES TO SEARCH (BOOKS OR CD-ROMS)

EBSCO Magazine Article Summaries
InfoTrac
NewsBank and other newspaper indexes
Readers' Guide to Periodical Literature
SIRS (Social Issues Resources Series)
WILSONDISC

## ONLINE DATABASES TO SEARCH

America Online
CompuServe

Dialog
Internet
Prodigy

## KEY WORDS AND DESCRIPTORS FOR PERIODICAL INDEX AND ONLINE SEARCHES

Public welfare
Public welfare reform
Welfare recipients
Public aid
Workfare
Aid to families with dependent children (AFDC)

## VIDEOTAPE ON THIS TOPIC

*Welfare Policy: Where Is It Headed.* Phase II Productions, 1989.

## FICTION BOOK RELATING TO TOPIC

Wolf, Virginia Euwer. *Make Lemonade.*

## SUGGESTIONS FOR NARROWING THIS TOPIC

Analyze a specific federal entitlement program; e.g., Workfare, food stamps, aid to families with dependent children (AFDC).
Discuss the moral and ethical aspects of welfare.
Investigate the special problems of women on welfare.
Research the subsidized housing issue. Use housing in your own town as an example.

## SUGGESTIONS FOR RELATED TOPICS

Daycare
Homelessness
Immigration
Health care reform
Social Security reform
Teenage pregnancy

This RESEARCH TOPIC GUIDE is intended to help the library user find information and materials on a particular topic in many sources throughout the library. Resources on this topic are not limited to those described and availability will depend upon the individual library. Feel free to ask a librarian for assistance.

# Women Clergy

## BACKGROUND

Although the numbers of women clergy have been increasing, much disagreement on this issue still exists. Most Protestant denominations have removed the barriers to ordination of women. Yet the Catholic, Islam, and Orthodox Jewish religions do not permit women to hold religious office. Those who support women clergy feel that they bring a new perspective and a personal style of ministry to the churches in which they serve.

## BROWSE FOR BOOKS ON THE SHELF USING THESE CALL NUMBERS

253.2
261.83
262.12
283.73

## LOOK UNDER THE FOLLOWING SUBJECTS IN THE CATALOG (CARD OR COMPUTER)

Women clergy
Women priests
Ordination of women
Women in Christianity

## REFERENCE MATERIALS THAT MAY HELP (BOOKS OR CD-ROMS)

*CQ Researcher*, September 8, 1995.
*Editorials on File*, Facts on File.
*Facts on File*
Reid, Daniel G., ed. *Dictionary of Christianity in America*, 1990.

## PERIODICAL INDEXES TO SEARCH (BOOKS OR CD-ROMS)

EBSCO Magazine Article Summaries
InfoTrac
NewsBank and other newspaper indexes
Readers' Guide to Periodical Literature
SIRS (Social Issues Resources Series)
WILSONDISC

## ONLINE DATABASES TO SEARCH

America Online
CompuServe

Dialog
Internet
Prodigy

## KEY WORDS AND DESCRIPTORS FOR PERIODICAL INDEX AND ONLINE SEARCHES

Women clergy
Ordination of women
Women priests
Women rabbis

## NATIONAL ORGANIZATION TO CONTACT FOR ADDITIONAL INFORMATION

Commission on the Status and Role of Women, 1200 Davis St., Evanston, IL 60201.

## SUGGESTIONS FOR NARROWING THIS TOPIC

Evaluate possible differences in approach to the ministry between men and women.
Investigate the impact of women clergy on the church service, on relations with congregation.
Research the historic role of women in the church.
What is the "stained glass ceiling" and its meaning to women clergy?

## SUGGESTIONS FOR RELATED TOPICS

Glass ceiling
Feminism and the church
Nuns
Women theologians

This RESEARCH TOPIC GUIDE is intended to help the library user find information and materials on a particular topic in many sources throughout the library. Resources on this topic are not limited to those described and availability will depend upon the individual library. Feel free to ask a librarian for assistance.

# Youth Gangs

## BACKGROUND

Street gangs are active in many of America's cities, promoting and perpetuating violence and fear. The causes are often attributed to racism, economic status, and illegal drug activities. Experts in the field are searching for effective methods of dealing with teenage gang violence, one of our most desperate social problems.

## BROWSE FOR BOOKS ON THE SHELF USING THESE CALL NUMBERS

364.1–364.106
302.34

## LOOK UNDER THE FOLLOWING SUBJECTS IN THE CATALOG (CARD OR COMPUTER)

Gangs
Gangs—United States
Violence—United States

## REFERENCE MATERIALS THAT MAY HELP (BOOKS OR CD-ROMS)

Corsini, Raymond J., ed. *Encyclopedia of Psychology*, 1994.
*CQ Researcher*, October 11, 1991.
*Facts on File*
Knox, George W. *National Gangs Resource Handbook: An Encyclopedic Reference*, 1995.

## PERIODICAL INDEXES TO SEARCH (BOOKS OR CD-ROMS)

EBSCO Magazine Article Summaries
InfoTrac
NewsBank and other newspaper indexes
Readers' Guide to Periodical Literature
SIRS (Social Issues Resources Series)
WILSONDISC

## ONLINE DATABASES TO SEARCH

America Online
CompuServe
Dialog

Internet

Prodigy

## KEY WORDS AND DESCRIPTORS FOR PERIODICAL INDEX AND ONLINE SEARCHES

Gangs

Teenage gangs

Women in gangs

Youth and firearms

## VIDEOTAPES ON THIS TOPIC

*American Me*. MCA Universal Home Video, 1992.

*Boyz in the Hood*. Columbia TriStar Home Video, 1992.

*Fort Apache, the Bronx*. Vestron Video, 1982.

*West Side Story*. CBS/Fox Video, 1984.

## FICTION BOOKS RELATING TO TOPIC

Bonham, Frank. *Durango Street*, 1983.

Hinton, S. E. *The Outsiders*, 1967.

Myers, Walter Dean. *Scorpions*, 1988.

Peck, Richard. *Bel-Air Bambi and the Mall Rats*, 1993.

## SUGGESTIONS FOR NARROWING THIS TOPIC

Evaluate the depiction of gangs in motion pictures and television.

Find out the symbols of gang membership and discuss their importance.

Report on a particular city; e.g., gangs in New York, Los Angeles.

Research a specific gang; e.g., Black Disciples, Bloods, Crips, Hell's Angels.

## SUGGESTIONS FOR RELATED TOPICS

Gang rape

Graffiti

Harley subculture

School violence

This RESEARCH TOPIC GUIDE is intended to help the library user find information and materials on a particular topic in many sources throughout the library. Resources on this topic are not limited to those described and availability will depend upon the individual library. Feel free to ask a librarian for assistance.

# III

# Social Studies Research Topic Guides

# Assassination of President John F. Kennedy

**BACKGROUND**

Thirty-fifth president of the United States, John F. Kennedy was assassinated in Dallas, Texas, on November 22, 1963. This popular young president had shown great leadership and potential during his brief time in office. Two days after the assassination, Lee Harvey Oswald, arrested for the crime, was shot and killed by Jack Ruby. Much controversy continues to surround these events.

**BROWSE FOR BOOKS ON THE SHELF USING THESE CALL NUMBERS**

Biography section under Kennedy, John F.
973.922–973.92209
364.1524

**LOOK UNDER THE FOLLOWING SUBJECTS IN THE CATALOG (CARD OR COMPUTER)**

Kennedy, John F. (John Fitzgerald), 1917–1963—Assassination
Kennedy, John F. (John Fitzgerald), 1917–1963—Death and burial
United States—Warren Commission
Oswald, Lee Harvey
Ruby, Jack

**REFERENCE MATERIALS THAT MAY HELP (BOOKS OR CD-ROMS)**

Magill, Frank N., ed. *Great Events from History: American Series*, 1975.
Meagher, Sylvia. *Master Index to the J.F.K. Assassination Investigation*, 1980.
United States. *Report of the Select Committee on Assassinations, U. S. House of Representatives, Ninety-fifth Congress, Second Session: Findings and Recommendations*, 1979.
United States. *The Warren Commission Report: The Official Report of the President's Commission on the Assassination of President Kennedy*, 1992.

**PERIODICAL INDEXES TO SEARCH (BOOKS OR CD-ROMS)**

EBSCO Magazine Article Summaries
InfoTrac
NewsBank and other newspaper indexes
Readers' Guide to Periodical Literature
WILSONDISC

**ONLINE DATABASES TO SEARCH**

America Online
CompuServe
Dialog

Internet
Prodigy

## KEY WORDS AND DESCRIPTORS FOR PERIODICAL INDEX AND ONLINE SEARCHES

Kennedy, John F.—assassination
Presidents—assassination
Oswald, Lee Harvey
Ruby, Jack
Warren Commission

## VIDEOTAPES ON THIS TOPIC

*Four Days in November*. MGM/UA Home Video, 1988.
*The Plot to Kill JFK: Rush to Judgement*. MPI Home Video, 1988.
*Reasonable Doubt: The Single Bullet Theory and the Assassination of John F. Kennedy*. White Star, 1988.

## FICTION BOOKS RELATING TO TOPIC

Gross, Virginia T. *The President Is Dead: A Story of the Kennedy Assassination*, 1993.
Ions, Edmund S. *Sherlock Holmes in Dallas*, 1980.

## NATIONAL ORGANIZATIONS TO CONTACT FOR ADDITIONAL INFORMATION

JFK Assassination Information Center, 603 Munger Ave., P.O. Box 70, Dallas, TX 75202.
John F. Kennedy Presidential Library—Museum, Columbia Point, Boston, MA 02125.

## SUGGESTIONS FOR NARROWING THIS TOPIC

Analyze one or more of the theories surrounding the assassination; e.g., role of CIA , Mafia, or KGB, single-bullet theory.
Discuss the findings of the Warren Commission.
Examine a key personality in the event; e.g., Lee Harvey Oswald, Jack Ruby, Governor John B. Connolly, Jr., Jacqueline Kennedy, Lyndon Johnson.

## SUGGESTIONS FOR RELATED TOPICS

Assassination of Robert Kennedy, Malcolm X, Abraham Lincoln, or Martin Luther King, Jr.
Investigate famous assassins in history; e.g., John Wilkes Booth, Sirhan Sirhan.

This RESEARCH TOPIC GUIDE is intended to help the library user find information and materials on a particular topic in many sources throughout the library. Resources on this topic are not limited to those described and availability will depend upon the individual library. Feel free to ask a librarian for assistance.

# Civil Rights Movement

**BACKGROUND**

Since the Civil Rights Act of 1957, the government has instituted measures to attempt to eradicate discrimination in the United States. School segregation, voting rights, equal employment, and other issues have been debated in the legislature with varying degrees of success. Important leaders in the civil rights movement include Martin Luther King, Jr., Malcolm X, John F. Kennedy, and Lyndon Johnson, among many others.

**BROWSE FOR BOOKS ON THE SHELF USING THESE CALL NUMBERS**

> 973.92
> 973.0496
> 323.4–323.4092
> 323.119–323.1196

**LOOK UNDER THE FOLLOWING SUBJECTS IN THE CATALOG (CARD OR COMPUTER)**

> Afro-Americans–Civil rights
> Civil rights movements—United States —History–20th century
> Civil rights—United States
> Civil rights workers
> United States—Race relations

**REFERENCE MATERIALS THAT MAY HELP (BOOKS OR CD-ROMS)**

> Magill, Frank H. *Great Events from History II: Human Rights Series*, 1992.
> Ploski, Harry A., and James Williams, ed. *The Negro Almanac: A Reference Work on the African American*, 1989.
> Smythe, Mabel M., ed. *The Black American Reference Book*, 1976.
> Williams, Michael W., ed. *The African American Encyclopedia*, 1993.
> Wexler, Sanford. *The Civil Rights Movement*, 1993.
> General encyclopedias

**PERIODICAL INDEXES TO SEARCH (BOOKS OR CD-ROMS)**

> EBSCO Magazine Article Summaries
> InfoTrac
> NewsBank and other newspaper indexes
> Readers' Guide to Periodical Literature
> SIRS (Social Issues Resources Series)
> WILSONDISC

**ONLINE DATABASES TO SEARCH**

> Dialog
> Internet

## KEY WORDS AND DESCRIPTORS FOR PERIODICAL INDEX AND ONLINE SEARCHES

Civil rights
Civil rights movements
Civil rights workers
Black history
Afro-American history

## VIDEOTAPES ON THIS TOPIC

*Martin Luther King Commemorative*. MPI Home Video, 1988.
*We Shall Overcome: A History of the Civil Rights Movement*. PBS Home Video, 1990.

## FICTION BOOKS RELATING TO TOPIC

Davis, Ossie. *Just like Martin*, 1992.
Ellison, Ralph. *Invisible Man*, 1952.
Forman, James. *Freedom's Blood*, 1979.
Moore, Yvette. *Freedom Songs*, 1991.

## NATIONAL ORGANIZATIONS TO CONTACT FOR ADDITIONAL INFORMATION

NAACP (National Association for the Advancement of Colored People), 4805 Mt. Hope Dr., Baltimore, MD 21215.
ACLU (Americans for Civil Liberty Union), 132 W. 43rd St., New York, NY 10036.

## SUGGESTIONS FOR NARROWING THIS TOPIC

Choose a particular civil rights leader to report on; e.g., Jesse Jackson, Roy Wilkins, Ida B. Wells-Barnett, Martin Luther King, Jr.
Research a historic civil rights incident; e.g., 1963 March on Washington, Greensboro sit-in, Rosa Parks and the Montgomery Bus Boycott.
Discuss the Southern Christian Leadership Conference or the NAACP.

## SUGGESTIONS FOR RELATED TOPICS

Anti-apartheid movement
Assassination of Martin Luther King, Jr.
Black power movement
Fourteenth Amendment to the Constitution
Ku Klux Klan
Racism

This RESEARCH TOPIC GUIDE is intended to help the library user find information and materials on a particular topic in many sources throughout the library. Resources on this topic are not limited to those described and availability will depend upon the individual library. Feel free to ask a librarian for assistance.

# Conclusion of the Cold War

**BACKGROUND**

Following World War II, antagonism developed between the Communist bloc countries and the free world. Major political and moral differences, especially between the United States and the Soviet Union, led to the buildup of nuclear weapons on both sides and an atmosphere of tension, hostility, and fear. In 1985, with the emergence of enlightened Soviet leadership, relations improved and the Cold War was on its way out.

**BROWSE FOR BOOKS ON THE SHELF USING THESE CALL NUMBERS**

> 327.73–327.73047
> 361.23
> 303.4827

**LOOK UNDER THE FOLLOWING SUBJECTS IN THE CATALOG (CARD OR COMPUTER)**

> United States—Foreign relations—1989–1993
> Soviet Union—Foreign relations—1985–1991
> Detente
> Cold War

**USE PAMPHLET FILE (ALSO CALLED VERTICAL FILE) UNDER THE HEADINGS**

> Soviet Union
> Russia

**REFERENCE MATERIALS THAT MAY HELP (BOOKS OR CD-ROMS)**

> Arms, Thomas S. *Encyclopedia of the Cold War*, 1994.
> Parrish, Thomas. *The Cold War Encyclopedia*, 1995.
> General encyclopedias

**PERIODICAL INDEXES TO SEARCH (BOOKS OR CD-ROMS)**

> EBSCO Magazine Article Summaries
> InfoTrac
> NewsBank and other newspaper indexes
> SIRS (Social Issues Resources Series)
> WILSONDISC

**ONLINE DATABASES TO SEARCH**

> America Online
> CompuServe

Dialog

Internet

Prodigy

## KEY WORDS AND DESCRIPTORS FOR PERIODICAL INDEX AND ONLINE SEARCHES

Post–Cold War

New world order

Geopolitics

World politics

U.S. foreign relations

Russian foreign relations

Soviet foreign relations

## VIDEOTAPES ON THIS TOPIC

*The Cold War: Europe and the Third World.* WGBH and Metropolitan Museum, 1989.

*U.S.-Soviet Relations.* Close Up Foundation, 1988.

## NATIONAL ORGANIZATIONS TO CONTACT FOR ADDITIONAL INFORMATION

American Committee on U.S.-Soviet Relations, 109 11th St., S.E., Washington, DC 20003.

Department of State, Office of Public Communication, Public Information Service, Bureau of Public Affairs, Rm. 4827A, Washington, DC 20520.

## SUGGESTIONS FOR NARROWING THIS TOPIC

Choose a superpower and discuss its impact on the Post–Cold War era; e.g., Japan, Russia, Germany.

Define and discuss several of the terms associated with the end of the Cold War; e.g., detente, glasnost, perestroika.

Investigate the arms control situation at the end of the Cold War.

What has been the role of the United Nations in bringing the Cold War to an end?

## SUGGESTIONS FOR RELATED TOPICS

George Bush

Independent republics of the former Soviet Union

Mikhail S. Gorbachev

Reuniting of East and West Germany

This RESEARCH TOPIC GUIDE is intended to help the library user find information and materials on a particular topic in many sources throughout the library. Resources on this topic are not limited to those described and availability will depend upon the individual library. Feel free to ask a librarian for assistance.

# Ethnic Conflict

**BACKGROUND**

Ethnic conflict is occurring all around the globe. From Sudan, South Africa, and Afghanistan to Armenia, Bosnia, and the Middle East, from Brazil and Peru to many cities in the United States, people of different ethnic backgrounds are at war with one another. Sometimes the reasons for their hostilities are shrouded in history. Often the struggles involve religion and power. Whatever the original cause, bitter ethnic hatred has caused death, heartache and despair.

**BROWSE FOR BOOKS ON THE SHELF USING THESE CALL NUMBERS**

> 301.451
> 305.8
> 306.8
> 320.54

**LOOK UNDER THE FOLLOWING SUBJECTS IN THE CATALOG (CARD OR COMPUTER)**

> Ethnic relations
> Ethnic groups
> Ethnicity
> Nationalism
> Culture conflict

**REFERENCE MATERIALS THAT MAY HELP (BOOKS OR CD-ROMS)**

> *CQ Researcher*, March 24, 1991.
> *Facts on File*
> Jones, Emrys, ed. *The Marshall Cavendish New Illustrated Encyclopedia of the World and Its People*, 1994.
> Magill, Frank N., ed. *Great Events from History II: Human Rights Series*, 1992.
> *Worldmark Encyclopedia of the Nations*. J. Wiley, 1995.
> General encyclopedias

**PERIODICAL INDEXES TO SEARCH (BOOKS OR CD-ROMS)**

> EBSCO Magazine Article Summaries
> InfoTrac
> NewsBank and other newspaper indexes
> Readers' Guide to Periodical Literature
> SIRS (Social Issues Resources)
> WILSONDISC

**ONLINE DATABASES TO SEARCH**

> America Online
> CompuServe

Dialog
Internet
Prodigy

## KEY WORDS AND DESCRIPTORS FOR PERIODICAL INDEX AND ONLINE SEARCHES

Nationalism
Ethnic conflict
Ethnic relations
Culture conflict
Bosnians, Serbs, Kurds, etc.

## VIDEOTAPE ON THIS TOPIC

*Power of One*. Warner Home Video, 1992.

## FICTION BOOKS RELATING TO TOPIC

Hesse, Karen. *Letters from Rifka*, 1992.
Laird, Elizabeth. *Kiss the Dust*, 1992.
Rochman, Hazel. *Somehow Tenderness Survives*, 1988.

## NATIONAL ORGANIZATIONS TO CONTACT FOR ADDITIONAL INFORMATION

Campaign for Peace and Democracy, P.O. Box 1640, New York, NY 10025.
Human Rights Watch, 485 Fifth Ave., New York, NY 10017–6104.
Project on Ethnic Relations, One Palmer Square, Ste. 435, Princeton, NJ 08542.

## SUGGESTIONS FOR NARROWING THIS TOPIC

Choose a specific ethnic conflict to discuss; e.g., Bosnia, Kurds, ethnic groups within the former Soviet Union, Middle East.
Consider the causes of ethnic conflict.
Research ethnic conflict within the United States

## SUGGESTIONS FOR RELATED TOPICS

Anti-Semitism
Cultural diversity
Hate groups
Immigration
Racism

This RESEARCH TOPIC GUIDE is intended to help the library user find information and materials on a particular topic in many sources throughout the library. Resources on this topic are not limited to those described and availability will depend upon the individual library. Feel free to ask a librarian for assistance.

# The Holocaust

## BACKGROUND

The Holocaust, also called Hitler's Final Solution, was the systematic genocide of the Jewish people and certain minority groups, such as Gypsies and homosexuals. Between 1941 and 1945 these people were transported to concentration camps, where over 5 million were put to death. Many others died from illness and malnutrition. At the end of World War II, Allied forces liberated the death camps.

## BROWSE FOR BOOKS ON THE SHELF USING THESE CALL NUMBERS

940.53–940.5315

## LOOK UNDER THE FOLLOWING SUBJECTS IN THE CATALOG (CARD OR COMPUTER)

Holocaust, Jewish (1939–1945)
Holocaust, Jewish (1939–1945)—Personal narratives
Many other subjects beginning Holocaust, Jewish (1939–1945)
World War, 1939–1945—Atrocities

## USE PAMPHLET FILE (ALSO CALLED VERTICAL FILE) UNDER THE HEADING

Holocaust

## REFERENCE MATERIALS THAT MAY HELP (BOOKS OR CD-ROMS)

Gilbert, Martin. *Atlas of the Holocaust*, 1993.
Gutman, Israel. *Encyclopedia of the Holocaust*, 1990.
Szonyi, David, ed. *The Holocaust: An Annotated Bibliography and Resource Guide*, 1985.
General encyclopedias

## PERIODICAL INDEXES TO SEARCH (BOOKS OR CD-ROMS)

EBSCO Magazine Article Summaries
InfoTrac
NewsBank and other newspaper indexes
Readers' Guide to Periodical Literature
SIRS (Social Issues Resources Series)
WILSONDISC

## ONLINE DATABASES TO SEARCH

Dialog
Internet

## KEY WORDS AND DESCRIPTORS FOR PERIODICAL INDEX AND ONLINE SEARCHES

Holocaust
Concentration camps
Jewish Holocaust

## VIDEOTAPES ON THIS TOPIC

*Schindler's List*. MCA Universal, 1994.
*Shoah*. Paramount Home Video, 1985.

## FICTION BOOKS RELATING TO TOPIC

Dillon, Ellis. *Children of Bach*, 1992.
Kerr, M. E. *Gentlehands*, 1978.
Matas, Carol. *Daniel's Story*, 1993.
Orlev, Uri. *The Island on Bird Street*, 1984.

## NATIONAL ORGANIZATIONS TO CONTACT FOR ADDITIONAL INFORMATION

Holocaust Documentation and Education Center, Inc., FIU–North Campus, 3000 N.E. 145th St., North Miami, FL 33181.

Holocaust Resource Center, Kean College of New Jersey Library, Union, New Jersey 07083.

Simon Wiesenthal Center, 9760 W. Pico Blvd., Los Angeles, CA 90035–4792.

## SUGGESTIONS FOR NARROWING THIS TOPIC

Choose an individual important in the Holocaust to write about; e.g., Anne Frank, Eli Wiesel, Joseph Mengele.

Describe what life might have been like for concentration camp inmates.

Learn about one or more famous rescuers of Jews; e.g., Raoul Wallenberg, Miep Gies.

What was Hitler's Final Solution?

## SUGGESTIONS FOR RELATED TOPICS

Anti-Semitism
Children of Holocaust survivors
Days of Remembrance
Ethnic cleansing or genocide
Nazi hunters
Zionism

This RESEARCH TOPIC GUIDE is intended to help the library user find information and materials on a particular topic in many sources throughout the library. Resources on this topic are not limited to those described and availability will depend upon the individual library. Feel free to ask a librarian for assistance.

# Immigration

## BACKGROUND

The social, legal, and economic impact of continuing heavy immigration of foreign nationals to the United States is under discussion in local, state, and federal arenas. Immigrants come from many cultures and arrive with diverse capabilities and educational backgrounds. Those who are prepared for work become mainstreamed and are a benefit to society. Those who have few skills or financial means and difficulty learning English often become dependents at great expense to the system. A nation of immigrants itself, the United States is searching for the best course to follow regarding the regulation of immigration.

## BROWSE FOR BOOKS ON THE SHELF USING THESE CALL NUMBERS

325.73
304.809

## LOOK UNDER THE FOLLOWING SUBJECTS IN THE CATALOG (CARD OR COMPUTER)

United States—Emigration and immigration
United States—Emigration and immigration—Biography
United States—Emigration and immigration—Government policy

## REFERENCE MATERIALS THAT MAY HELP (BOOKS OR CD-ROMS)

Bogue, Donald J. *The Population of the United States: Historical Trends and Future Projections*, 1985.
*CQ Researcher*, February 3, 1995.
Thernstrom, Stephen, ed. *Harvard Encyclopedia of American Ethnic Groups*, 1980.
U.S. Bureau of the Census. *Statistical Abstracts of the United States, 1995*.
General encyclopedias

## PERIODICAL INDEXES TO SEARCH (BOOKS OR CD-ROMS)

EBSCO Magazine Article Summaries
InfoTrac
NewsBank and other newspaper indexes
Readers' Guide to Periodical Literature
WILSONDISC

## ONLINE DATABASES TO SEARCH

America Online
CompuServe
Dialog
Internet
Prodigy

## KEY WORDS AND DESCRIPTORS FOR PERIODICAL INDEX AND ONLINE SEARCHES

Immigration and emigration
Immigration and emigration law
Immigrants
Alien labor
Illegal aliens

## VIDEOTAPES ON THIS TOPIC

*The Immigrant Experience: A Story of the American Dream.* Learning Co. of America, 1992.

*The Immigrant Experience: The Long, Long Journey.* Learning Co. of America, 1986.

## FICTION BOOKS RELATING TO TOPIC

Geras, Adele. *Voyage*, 1983.
Hesse, Karen. *Letters from Rifka*, 1992.
Levitin, Sonia. *Silver Days*, 1989.
Tan, Amy. *Joy Luck Club*, 1989.
Yep, Lawrence. *Mountain Light*, 1985.

## NATIONAL ORGANIZATIONS TO CONTACT FOR ADDITIONAL INFORMATION

Center for Immigration Studies, 1815 H St., N.W., Ste. 1010, Washington, DC 20006.

Federation for American Immigration Reform, 1666 Connecticut Ave., N.W., Ste. 400, Washington, DC 20009.

Statue of Liberty National Monument and Ellis Island, Liberty Island, New York, NY 10004.

## SUGGESTIONS FOR NARROWING THIS TOPIC

Choose a specific nationality that has immigrated to the United States and discuss its history and current status.

Discuss the changing patterns of immigration.

Research immigration reform in the United States.

Select a particular state or area of the country and report on immigration status; e.g., Florida, California, New York.

## SUGGESTIONS FOR RELATED TOPICS

English as the national language
Expatriots
Illegal aliens
Political refugees
Refugee Act of 1980

This RESEARCH TOPIC GUIDE is intended to help the library user find information and materials on a particular topic in many sources throughout the library. Resources on this topic are not limited to those described and availability will depend upon the individual library. Feel free to ask a librarian for assistance.

# Independent Republics of the Former Soviet Union

**BACKGROUND**

Once a world superpower, the Soviet Union collapsed in 1991 as its individual states declared independence. These new nations differ from each other culturally, geographically, historically, economically, and politically. Their ethnic makeup, language, and religion varies. The world is watching as these new entities struggle to become nations.

**BROWSE FOR BOOKS ON THE SHELF USING THESE CALL NUMBERS**

> 947–947.085
>
> 914.7
>
> Look up call numbers for each republic.

**LOOK UNDER THE FOLLOWING SUBJECTS IN THE CATALOG (CARD OR COMPUTER)**

> Former Soviet republics
>
> Commonwealth of Independent States
>
> Look under each republic; e.g., Azerbaijan, Armenia, Belarus, Estonia, Georgia, Kazakhstan, Kyrgyzstan, Latvia, Lithuania, Moldova, Russia, Tajikistan, Turkmenistan, Ukraine, Uzbekistan.

**USE PAMPHLET FILE (ALSO CALLED VERTICAL FILE) UNDER THE HEADINGS**

> Each republic may have its own heading or be grouped under Independent Republics

**REFERENCE MATERIALS THAT MAY HELP (BOOKS OR CD-ROMS)**

> Batalden, Stephen K., and Sandra L. Batalden. *The Newly Independent States of Eurasia: Handbook of Former Soviet Republics*, 1994.
>
> Brawer, Moshe. *Atlas of Russia and the Independent Republics*, 1995.
>
> *CQ Researcher*, July 12, 1991.
>
> *Facts on File*
>
> Shoemaker, M. Wesley. *Russia, Eurasian States, and Eastern Europe, 1995*, 1995.
>
> United States. Department of State. *Background Notes*.
>
> General encyclopedias

**PERIODICAL INDEXES TO SEARCH (BOOKS OR CD-ROMS)**

> EBSCO Magazine Article Summaries
>
> InfoTrac
>
> NewsBank and other newspaper indexes
>
> Readers' Guide to Periodical Literature

SIRS (Social Issues Resources Series)
WILSONDISC

## ONLINE DATABASES TO SEARCH

America Online
CompuServe
Dialog
Internet
Prodigy

## KEY WORDS AND DESCRIPTORS FOR PERIODICAL INDEX AND ONLINE SEARCHES

Search using the name of a specific republic; e.g., Latvia, Russia, Estonia.
Commonwealth of Independent States
Former Soviet Union

## VIDEOTAPE ON THIS TOPIC

*Russia Then and Now.* Clay Francisco Films, 1994.

## NATIONAL ORGANIZATIONS TO CONTACT FOR ADDITIONAL INFORMATION

Contact a specific embassy (see U.S. Department of State Diplomatic List
   for complete listing):
   Embassy of the Russian Federation, 1125 16th St., N.W., Washington,
   DC 20036.
Embassy of Ukraine, 3350 M St., N.W., Washington, DC 20007.

## SUGGESTIONS FOR NARROWING THIS TOPIC

Choose a specific republic and research one or more of the following: culture,
   economic aspects, geography, history, politics, future prospects.
Comment on relations between the United States and the independent republics.
Discuss one or more of the important political figures; e.g., Boris Yeltzin,
   Mikhail Gorbachev.
Investigate the ethnic conflict within and between the new republics.

## SUGGESTIONS FOR RELATED TOPICS

Collapse of the Soviet Union
End of the Cold War
Ethnic conflict

This RESEARCH TOPIC GUIDE is intended to help the library user find information and
materials on a particular topic in many sources throughout the library. Resources on this
topic are not limited to those described and availability will depend upon the individual
library. Feel free to ask a librarian for assistance.

# McCarthy Hearings

## BACKGROUND

On February 9, 1950, Senator Joseph R. McCarthy, a Republican from Wisconsin, publicly charged that at least 205 Department of State employees were Communists, traitors, and spies. This accusation touched a deep sense of fear among many Americans that the Communists were infiltrating the country and would eventually take over. Congress investigated the charges, and hearings were conducted during which many innocent people lost their livelihoods and reputations.

## BROWSE FOR BOOKS ON THE SHELF USING THESE CALL NUMBERS

973.918
335.4
353.6
320.973
Biography section under McCarthy, Joseph

## LOOK UNDER THE FOLLOWING SUBJECTS IN THE CATALOG (CARD OR COMPUTER)

McCarthy, Joseph—1908–1957
Communism—United States
McCarthy-Army controversy, 1954
Subversive activities—United States
Anti-communist movements—United States

## REFERENCE MATERIALS THAT MAY HELP (BOOKS OR CD-ROMS)

Commager, Henry Steele, et al. *The American Destiny*, 1976.
Hochman, Stanley, and Eleanor Hochman. *A Dictionary of Contemporary American History: 1945 to the Present*, 1993.
Magill, Frank N., ed. *Great Events from History: American History Series*, 1975.

## PERIODICAL INDEXES TO SEARCH (BOOKS OR CD-ROMS)

EBSCO Magazine Article Summaries
InfoTrac
NewsBank and other newspaper indexes
Readers' Guide to Periodical Literature
SIRS (Social Issues Resources Series)
WILSONDISC

## ONLINE DATABASES TO SEARCH

Dialog
Internet

## KEY WORDS AND DESCRIPTORS FOR PERIODICAL INDEX AND ONLINE SEARCHES

McCarthy, Joseph
Communists—investigations
Anti-Communist movements
McCarthy witch hunt trials
McCarthy hearings
McCarthy-army controversy

## VIDEOTAPE ON THIS TOPIC

*McCarthy: Death of a Witch Hunter.* MPI Home Video, 1986.

## NATIONAL ORGANIZATION TO CONTACT FOR ADDITIONAL INFORMATION

Joseph R. McCarthy Foundation, P.O. Box 8040, Appleton, WI 54913.

## SUGGESTIONS FOR NARROWING THIS TOPIC

Assess the role of television in the McCarthy hearings.
Discuss the impact of the McCarthy hearings on civil liberties.
Report on a key personality in these events; e.g., Alger Hiss, Klaus Fuchs, Margaret Chase Smith, Roy Cohn.
What were McCarthy's political motives?

## SUGGESTIONS FOR RELATED TOPICS

American Communist party
Cold War
Red Scare
Rosenberg Case
Voice of America

This RESEARCH TOPIC GUIDE is intended to help the library user find information and materials on a particular topic in many sources throughout the library. Resources on this topic are not limited to those described and availability will depend upon the individual library. Feel free to ask a librarian for assistance.

# Peace Corps

## BACKGROUND

Introduced by John F. Kennedy in 1961, the Peace Corps is an organization devoted to placing volunteers into developing nations. These volunteer teachers, health workers, engineers, and agricultural workers help to improve the skills and quality of life for the native peoples while living among them. The primary goal of the Peace Corps is to promote world peace and to increase mutual understanding between Americans and the people of other nations.

## BROWSE FOR BOOKS ON THE SHELF USING THESE CALL NUMBERS

> 361.26
> 361.6
> 309.22

## LOOK UNDER THE FOLLOWING SUBJECTS IN THE CATALOG (CARD OR COMPUTER)

> Peace Corps (U.S.)
> Peace Corps (U.S.)—History

## USE PAMPHLET FILE (ALSO CALLED VERTICAL FILE) UNDER THE HEADING

> Peace Corps

## REFERENCE MATERIALS THAT MAY HELP (BOOKS OR CD-ROMS)

> *CQ Researcher*, January 25, 1991.
> Magill, Frank N., ed. *Great Events from History: American Series*, 1975.
> *Passbooks for Career Opportunities: Peace Corps Examination National Learning Corp.*, 1990.
> General encyclopedias

## PERIODICAL INDEXES TO SEARCH (BOOKS OR CD-ROMS)

> EBSCO Magazine Article Summaries
> InfoTrac
> NewsBank and other newspaper indexes
> Readers' Guide to Periodical Literature
> SIRS (Social Issues Resources Series)
> WILSONDISC

## ONLINE DATABASES TO SEARCH

Internet
Dialog

## KEY WORDS AND DESCRIPTORS FOR PERIODICAL INDEX AND ONLINE SEARCHES

U.S. Peace Corps
Peace Corps

## FICTION BOOK RELATING TO TOPIC

Smith, Mary-Ann Tiro. *Lament for a Silver-Eyed Woman*, 1987.

## NATIONAL ORGANIZATION TO CONTACT FOR ADDITIONAL INFORMATION

Peace Corps, 1990 K St., N.W., Washington, DC 20526.

## SUGGESTIONS FOR NARROWING THIS TOPIC

Analyze the Peace Corps program and its effectiveness.
How is the Peace Corps viewed by the nations in which it serves?
Investigate the origins of the Peace Corps.
Research personal narratives of Peace Corps volunteers.
Report on senior citizens in the Peace Corps.

## SUGGESTIONS FOR RELATED TOPICS

Americorps
City Year
National Service Program
VISTA (Volunteers in Service to America)

This RESEARCH TOPIC GUIDE is intended to help the library user find information and materials on a particular topic in many sources throughout the library. Resources on this topic are not limited to those described and availability will depend upon the individual library. Feel free to ask a librarian for assistance.

# Persian Gulf War
# (August 3, 1990–February 27, 1991)

## BACKGROUND

With Iraq's invasion of Kuwait on August 3, 1990, the United States moved to protect its economic interests in the Middle East by mobilizing American servicemen and women as well as reservists. Led by H. Norman Schwarzkopf, the Allied Forces won a victory over Saddam Hussein and his Revolutionary Command Council.

## BROWSE FOR BOOKS ON THE SHELF USING THESE CALL NUMBERS

956.7–956.7044

## LOOK UNDER THE FOLLOWING SUBJECTS IN THE CATALOG (CARD OR COMPUTER)

Persian Gulf War, 1991
Operation Desert Shield, 1990–1991
Operation Desert Storm, 1990–1991
Iraq-Kuwait crisis, 1990–1991

## USE PAMPHLET FILE (ALSO CALLED VERTICAL FILE) UNDER THE HEADING

Persian Gulf War

## REFERENCE MATERIALS THAT MAY HELP (BOOKS OR CD-ROMS)

Ali, Sheikh R. *Encyclopedia of the Persian Gulf War*, 1995.
*CQ Researcher*, March 15, 1991.
*Europa World Yearbook*
*Facts on File*
Summers, Harry G. *Persian Gulf War Almanac*, 1995.
United Nations. *Yearbook of the United Nations, 1991*, 1992.
General encyclopedias.

## PERIODICAL INDEXES TO SEARCH (BOOKS OR CD-ROMS)

EBSCO Magazine Article Summaries
InfoTrac
NewsBank and other newspaper indexes
Readers' Guide to Periodical Literature
SIRS (Social Issues Resources Series)
WILSONDISC

## ONLINE DATABASES TO SEARCH

Dialog
Internet

## KEY WORDS AND DESCRIPTORS FOR PERIODICAL INDEX AND ONLINE SEARCHES

Persian Gulf War
Iraq-Kuwait War
Iraq-Kuwait invasion
Operation Desert Storm
Operation Desert Shield
Persian Gulf crisis

## VIDEOTAPES ON THIS TOPIC

*CNN: War in the Gulf.* CNN Video, 1991.
*Desert Storm: The Victory.* Turner Home Entertainment, 1991.

## FICTION BOOKS RELATING TO TOPIC

Cooney, Caroline. *Operation: Homefront*, 1992.
Kerr, M. E. *Linger*, 1993

## SUGGESTIONS FOR NARROWING THIS TOPIC

Analyze the uses of censorship and propaganda.
Describe military equipment employed in the war.
Discuss the role of the media during the war.
Investigate the causes of the war.
Research the environmental impacts.
What is the Persian Gulf syndrome and its significance?

## SUGGESTIONS FOR RELATED TOPICS

Colin Powell
George Bush
H. Norman Schwarzkopf
Iraq
Kuwait
Saddam Hussein

This RESEARCH TOPIC GUIDE is intended to help the library user find information and materials on a particular topic in many sources throughout the library. Resources on this topic are not limited to those described and availability will depend upon the individual library. Feel free to ask a librarian for assistance.

# Underground Railroad

## BACKGROUND

Between the years 1830 and 1860 thousands of slaves escaped to freedom on the Underground Railroad. Consisting of a vast network of trails, safe houses, churches, and hideouts, the Underground Railroad provided routes from the southern slave states to the north and Canada. Many people, both black and white, served as conductors along the way.

## BROWSE FOR BOOKS ON THE SHELF USING THESE CALL NUMBERS

973.049–973.0496
973.711
326.0973

## LOOK UNDER THE FOLLOWING SUBJECTS IN THE CATALOG (CARD OR COMPUTER)

Underground railroad
Fugitive slaves—United States
Anti-slavery movements
Abolitionists

## USE PAMPHLET FILE (ALSO CALLED VERTICAL FILE) UNDER THE HEADING

Underground Railroad

## REFERENCE MATERIALS THAT MAY HELP (BOOKS OR CD-ROMS)

Adler, Mortimer J., ed. *The Negro in American History*, 1969.
Blockson, Charles L. *Hippocrene Guide to the Underground Railroad*, 1994.
Low, W. Augustus, and Virgil A. Clift, eds. *Encyclopedia of Black America*, 1984.
Williams, Michael W., ed. *African American Encyclopedia*, 1993.
General encyclopedias

## PERIODICAL INDEXES TO SEARCH (BOOKS OR CD-ROMS)

EBSCO Magazine Article Summaries
InfoTrac
Readers' Guide to Periodical Literature
SIRS (Social Issues Resources Series)
WILSONDISC

## ONLINE DATABASES TO SEARCH

Dialog
Internet

## KEY WORDS AND DESCRIPTORS FOR PERIODICAL INDEX AND ONLINE SEARCHES

Underground Railroad
Slavery
Abolition

## VIDEOTAPES ON THIS TOPIC

*Follow the Drinking Gourd: A Story of the Underground Railroad*. Rabbit Ears Production, 1992.
*Voice of the Fugitive*. National Film Board of Canada, 1978.

## FICTION BOOKS RELATING TO TOPIC

Armstrong, Jennifer. *Steal Away*, 1992.
Beatty, Patricia. *Jayhawker*, 1991.
———. *Who Comes with Cannons*, 1991.
Meltzer, Milton. *Underground Man*, 1972.
Stolz, Mary. *Cezanne Pinto: A Memoir*, 1994.

## NATIONAL ORGANIZATION TO CONTACT FOR ADDITIONAL INFORMATION

African-American History Association, P.O. Box 115268, Atlanta, GA 30310.

## SUGGESTIONS FOR NARROWING THIS TOPIC

Choose a particular route to describe.
Describe the procedure typically followed in helping a slave travel the Underground Railroad.
Investigate the development of the Underground Railroad.
Research the music and poetry of the Underground Railroad.
What was the role of the Quakers in the success of the Underground Railroad?
Write about one of the famous "conductors" or "passengers" on the Underground Railroad.

## SUGGESTIONS FOR RELATED TOPICS

Abolition movement
Civil rights movement
Frederick Douglass
Harriet Tubman
Levi Coffin

This RESEARCH TOPIC GUIDE is intended to help the library user find information and materials on a particular topic in many sources throughout the library. Resources on this topic are not limited to those described and availability will depend upon the individual library. Feel free to ask a librarian for assistance.

# Vietnam War (1961-1975)

**BACKGROUND**

Possibly the most controversial war in U.S. history, the Vietnam War pitted the Communist government of North Vietnam against the democratic government of South Vietnam. The U.S. role as South Vietnam's military advisor soon grew to include troop support and full involvement. By 1975, when the United States pulled out, over 46,000 Americans had been killed.

**BROWSE FOR BOOKS ON THE SHELF USING THESE CALL NUMBERS**

> 959
> 959.7–959.7043

**LOOK UNDER THE FOLLOWING SUBJECTS IN THE CATALOG (CARD OR COMPUTER)**

> Vietnamese Conflict, 1961–1975
> Many other subjects beginning Vietnamese conflict, 1961–1975

**USE PAMPHLET FILE (ALSO CALLED VERTICAL FILE) UNDER THE HEADING**

> Vietnamese conflict

**REFERENCE MATERIALS THAT MAY HELP (BOOKS OR CD-ROMS)**

> Bowman, John S., ed. *Vietnam War: An Almanac*, 1985.
> *Editorial Research Reports*, Facts on File.
> *Facts on File*
> Summers, Harry G. *The Vietnam War Almanac*, 1985.
> General encyclopedias

**PERIODICAL INDEXES TO SEARCH (BOOKS OR CD-ROMS)**

> EBSCO Magazine Article Summaries
> InfoTrac
> NewsBank and other newspaper indexes
> Readers' Guide to Periodical Literature
> SIRS (Social Issues Resources Series)
> WILSONDISC

**ONLINE DATABASES TO SEARCH**

> America Online
> CompuServe
> Dialog
> Internet
> Prodigy

## KEY WORDS AND DESCRIPTORS FOR PERIODICAL INDEX AND ONLINE SEARCHES

Vietnamese Conflict
Vietnam War

## VIDEOTAPES ON THIS TOPIC

*All the Unsung Heroes: The Vietnam Memorial*. Heritage America Group, 1991.
*Apocalpyse Now*. Paramount Home Video, 1981.
*Gardens of Stone*. CBS/Fox Video, 1987.
*Platoon*. HBO Video, 1986.
*Vietnam: A Chronicle of a War*. CBS/Fox Video, 1981.

## FICTION BOOKS RELATING TO TOPIC

Myers, Walter Dean. *Fallen Angels*, 1988.
Nelson, Theresa. *And One for All*, 1991.
Qualey, Marsha. *Come in from the Cold*, 1994.

## NATIONAL ORGANIZATIONS TO CONTACT FOR ADDITIONAL INFORMATION

Vietnam Veterans against the War, P.O. Box 408594, Chicago, IL 60640.
Vietnam Veterans of America, 1224 M St., N.W., Washington, DC 20005–5783.

## SUGGESTIONS FOR NARROWING THIS TOPIC

Describe the antiwar sentiment, protest movements, and draft resistors.
Discuss the moral and ethical aspects of the war.
Discuss military policy and/or choose a particular event to analyze; e.g., Tet Offensive, My Lai Massacre.
How has the war been portrayed in motion pictures?
Investigate the role of the media.

## SUGGESTIONS FOR RELATED TOPICS

Agent Orange
Conscientious objectors
MIAs/POWs
President Lyndon Johnson
Post–traumatic stress disorder
Vietnam War Memorial

This RESEARCH TOPIC GUIDE is intended to help the library user find information and materials on a particular topic in many sources throughout the library. Resources on this topic are not limited to those described and availability will depend upon the individual library. Feel free to ask a librarian for assistance.

# Watergate Affair

## BACKGROUND

Beginning with the breakin of the Democratic National Committee headquarters at the Watergate Hotel on June 17, 1972, by employees of the Committee to Reelect the President (Nixon), the Watergate affair took on a life of its own. Before it was finally over, when President Richard Nixon was forced to resign on August 9, 1974, many careers were ruined.

## BROWSE FOR BOOKS ON THE SHELF USING THESE CALL NUMBERS

364.132

973.924

324.27

342.73

345.73

Biography section under Nixon, Richard M. (and under any other key personalities in the affair)

## LOOK UNDER THE FOLLOWING SUBJECTS IN THE CATALOG (CARD OR COMPUTER)

Watergate affair, 1972–

Watergate affair, 1972–1974

Watergate trial, Washington, D.C., 1973

Other headings beginning with Watergate affair

United States—Politics and government—1969–1974

Nixon, Richard M. (Richard Milhous), 1913–1994

## REFERENCE MATERIALS THAT MAY HELP (BOOKS OR CD-ROMS)

Commager, Henry Steele, et al. *The American Destiny*, 1976.

Congressional Quarterly. *Watergate: Chronology of a Crisis*, 1973.

*Dictionary of American History*, Scribner's, 1976.

Foner, Eric, and John A. Garraty, eds. *The Reader's Companion to American History*, 1991.

Smith, Myron J. *Watergate: An Annotated Bibliography of Sources in English, 1972–1982*, 1983.

United States. Congress. Senate. Select Committee on Presidential Campaign Activities.

*Hearings: Watergate and Related Activities*, 1973.

## PERIODICAL INDEXES TO SEARCH (BOOKS OR CD-ROMS)

EBSCO Magazine Article Summaries

InfoTrac

NewsBank and other newspaper indexes
Readers' Guide to Periodical Literature
SIRS (Social Issues Resources Series)
WILSONDISC

## ONLINE DATABASES TO SEARCH

Dialog
Internet

## KEY WORDS AND DESCRIPTORS FOR PERIODICAL INDEX AND ONLINE SEARCHES

Watergate
Watergate affair
Watergate trial
Nixon, Richard
Use any of the key personalities in the affair; e.g., Charles Colson, John Dean, Sam Ervin.

## VIDEOTAPES ON THIS TOPIC

*All the President's Men*. Festival Films, 1976.
*Watergate Affair, 1972–1974*, Films for the Humanities, 1995.

## SUGGESTIONS FOR NARROWING THIS TOPIC

Assess the importance of the *Washington Post* in the outcome of the Watergate affair.
Discuss the significance of "deep throat," secret tape recordings, dirty tricks.
Investigate the possible involvement of the CIA.
Report on a significant personality involved in the affair; e.g., John Ehrlichman, Bob Haldeman, Richard Nixon, Leon Jaworski.

## SUGGESTIONS FOR RELATED TOPICS

Impeachment
Pentagon Papers
Political corruption
Vietnam War

This RESEARCH TOPIC GUIDE is intended to help the library user find information and materials on a particular topic in many sources throughout the library. Resources on this topic are not limited to those described and availability will depend upon the individual library. Feel free to ask a librarian for assistance.

# Witchcraft in Colonial America

**BACKGROUND**

During the end of the seventeenth century, hysteria swept through the New England colonies, particularly in Salem, Massachusetts, when people became convinced that some of their fellow citizens were witches. Many accused witches (usually women) were put on trial and some were subsequently executed.

**BROWSE FOR BOOKS ON THE SHELF USING THESE CALL NUMBERS**

> 133.4–133.43
> 345.744
> 974.4

**LOOK UNDER THE FOLLOWING SUBJECTS IN THE CATALOG (CARD OR COMPUTER)**

> Witchcraft—Massachusetts—Salem
> Salem (Mass.)—History
> Trials (Witchcraft)—Massachusetts—Salem
> Witchcraft—History
> Witchcraft—New England

**REFERENCE MATERIALS THAT MAY HELP (BOOKS OR CD-ROMS)**

> Guiley, Rosemary Ellen. *The Encyclopedia of Witches and Witchcraft*, 1990.
> Knappman, Edward W., ed. *Great American Trials*, 1994.
> Magill, Frank N., ed. *Great Events from History: American History Series*, 1975.
> *Mysteries of Mind, Space and Time: The Unexplained*. H. Stuttman, 1992.
> *Salem Witchcraft; with an Account of Salem Village and a History of Opinions on Witchcraft and Kindred Subjects*. Corner House, 1971.
> Robbins, Rossell H. *The Encyclopedia of Witchcraft and Demonology*, 1986.
> General encyclopedias

**PERIODICAL INDEXES TO SEARCH (BOOKS OR CD-ROMS)**

> EBSCO Magazine Article Summaries
> InfoTrac
> Readers' Guide to Periodical Literature
> SIRS (Social Issues Resources Series)
> WILSONDISC

**ONLINE DATABASES TO SEARCH**

> CompuServe
> Dialog
> Internet

# KEY WORDS AND DESCRIPTORS FOR PERIODICAL INDEX AND ONLINE SEARCHES

Witchcraft
Witchcraft trials
Salem, Massachusetts
Use the name of a key personality in the trials; e.g., Tituba, Cotton Mather.

# VIDEOTAPES ON THIS TOPIC

*Three Sovereigns for Sarah*. PBS Video, 1985.
*The Witches of Salem*. LCA, 1986.

# FICTION BOOKS RELATING TO TOPIC

Clapp, Patricia. *Witches' Children*, 1982.
Farber, Norma. *Mercy Short: A Winter Journal, North Boston, 1692–93*, 1982.
Rinaldi, Ann. *A Break with Charity: A Story about the Salem Witch Trials*, 1992.
Westall, Robert. *The Devil on the Road*, 1979.

# NATIONAL ORGANIZATIONS TO CONTACT FOR ADDITIONAL INFORMATION

Essex Institute, 132 Essex Street, Salem, MA 01970.
Historic Salem, Inc., P.O. Box 865, Salem, MA 01970.
Salem Witch Museum, 19 1/2 Washington Square N., Salem, MA 01970.

# SUGGESTIONS FOR NARROWING THIS TOPIC

Choose an important figure involved in the witch hunts to research; e.g., Tituba, Cotton Mather.
Choose a specific family that was affected by the witch hunts; e.g., Corey, Esty, Bilby, Bishop.
Describe the Salem witchcraft trials.
Discuss the origins of witchcraft.
Why did the witchcraft scare occur when and where it did?

# SUGGESTIONS FOR RELATED TOPICS

Hysteria
Modern day "witch hunts"; e.g., McCarthy witch hunts
Nostradamus
Role of women in Puritan society
Twentieth century witchcraft
Witchcraft in the Middle Ages

This RESEARCH TOPIC GUIDE is intended to help the library user find information and materials on a particular topic in many sources throughout the library. Resources on this topic are not limited to those described and availability will depend upon the individual library. Feel free to ask a librarian for assistance.

# Women's Rights Movement

## BACKGROUND

The women's rights movement may have begun with the 1961 President's Commission on the Status of Women headed by Eleanor Roosevelt, which reported that women were earning at least 40 percent less than men in comparable jobs. There followed key events and legislation such as the Civil Rights Act of 1964, the founding of the National Organization for Women (NOW), the introduction of the Equal Rights Amendment, and the *Roe vs. Wade* abortion decision. Concerned citizens continue to work toward true equality between the sexes.

## BROWSE FOR BOOKS ON THE SHELF USING THESE CALL NUMBERS

305.42
301.412

## LOOK UNDER THE FOLLOWING SUBJECTS IN THE CATALOG (CARD OR COMPUTER)

Women's rights
Feminism
Feminists
Sex discrimination against women

## USE PAMPHLET FILE (ALSO CALLED VERTICAL FILE) UNDER THE HEADING

Women's rights

## REFERENCE MATERIALS THAT MAY HELP (BOOKS OR CD-ROMS)

*CQ Researcher*, August 9, 1991; May 29, 1992; October 29, 1993.
McPhee, Carol, and Ann Fitzgerald, eds. *Feminist Quotations: Voices of Rebels, Reformers and Visionaries*, 1979.
Morgan, Robin, ed. *Sisterhood Is Global*, 1984.
General encyclopedias

## PERIODICAL INDEXES TO SEARCH (BOOKS OR CD-ROMS)

EBSCO Magazine Article Summaries
InfoTrac
Newsbank and other newspaper indexes
Readers' Guide to Periodical Literature
SIRS (Social Issues Resources Series)
WILSONDISC

## ONLINE DATABASES TO SEARCH

America Online
CompuServe
Dialog

Internet
Prodigy

## KEY WORDS AND DESCRIPTORS FOR PERIODICAL INDEX AND ONLINE SEARCHES

Women's movement
Women's rights
Feminism
Sex discrimination

## VIDEOTAPES ON THIS TOPIC

*Rookie of the Year*. Time-Life Films, 1975.
*Woman and Man*. Films for the Humanities, 1986.

## FICTION BOOKS RELATING TO TOPIC

Hunt, Irene. *Claws of a Young Century*, 1983.
Tolan, Stephanie E. *The Great Skinner Strike*, 1983.

## NATIONAL ORGANIZATIONS TO CONTACT FOR ADDITIONAL INFORMATION

MS Foundation for Women, 141 5th Ave., Ste. 6-S, New York, NY 10010.
National Organization for Women (NOW), 1000 16th St., N.W., Ste. 700, Washington, DC 20036.
National Women's Hall of Fame, 76 Fall St., Seneca Falls, NY 13148.

## SUGGESTIONS FOR NARROWING THIS TOPIC

Investigate women's rights in Saudi Arabia, India, Japan, or other country.
Relate the history of the women's rights movement.
Report on a contemporary woman active in women's rights; e.g., Gloria Steinem, Germaine Greer, Betty Friedan.
Report on a historic woman active in women's rights; e.g., Susan B. Anthony, Elizabeth Cady Stanton, Margaret Sanger.
Research the suffragette movement.

## SUGGESTIONS FOR RELATED TOPICS

Gay rights
Rights of teenagers
Sexual harassment
Women and sports

This RESEARCH TOPIC GUIDE is intended to help the library user find information and materials on a particular topic in many sources throughout the library. Resources on this topic are not limited to those described and availability will depend upon the individual library. Feel free to ask a librarian for assistance.

# Woodstock Festival

**BACKGROUND**

One of the largest counterculture events ever to explode on the American scene, Woodstock Festival opened in August 1969 on a farm in upstate New York, and an estimated 500,000 people flooded in for a weekend that would go down in history.

**BROWSE FOR BOOKS ON THE SHELF USING THESE CALL NUMBERS**

> 784–484.54
>
> Biography section under Hendrix, Jimi (and under other individuals and performing groups who appeared at Woodstock)

**LOOK UNDER THE FOLLOWING SUBJECTS IN THE CATALOG (CARD OR COMPUTER)**

> Woodstock Festival (1969: Bethel, New York)
> Rock music—History & criticism

**REFERENCE MATERIALS THAT MAY HELP (BOOKS OR CD-ROMS)**

> Wenner, Jann S., ed. *20 Years of Rolling Stone*, 1987.
> General encyclopedias

**PERIODICAL INDEXES TO SEARCH (BOOKS OR CD-ROMS)**

> EBSCO Magazine Article Summaries
> InfoTrac
> NewsBank and other newspaper indexes
> Readers' Guide to Periodical Literature
> SIRS (Social Issues Resources Series)
> WILSONDISC

**ONLINE DATABASES TO SEARCH**

> America Online
> CompuServe
> Dialog
> Internet
> Prodigy

**KEY WORDS AND DESCRIPTORS FOR PERIODICAL INDEX AND ONLINE SEARCHES**

> Woodstock
> Woodstock Festival

Rock music—history & criticism
Nineteen-sixties decade—music

## VIDEOTAPES ON THIS TOPIC

*Woodstock*. Festival Films, 1970.
*Woodstock: Three Days of Peace and Music*. Warner Home Video, 1970.

## FICTION BOOK RELATING TO TOPIC

Strasser, Todd. *Rock 'n' Roll Nights*, 1982.

## NATIONAL ORGANIZATIONS TO CONTACT FOR ADDITIONAL INFORMATION

Rhythm & Blues Rock & Roll Society, P.O. Box 1949, New Haven, CT 06510.
Rock and Roll Hall of Fame and Museum, 1 Key Plaza, Cleveland, OH 44115.

## SUGGESTIONS FOR NARROWING THIS TOPIC

Discuss the impact of the Woodstock Generation on American culture.
Discuss the music of Woodstock.
Report on a specific performer or group; e.g., Janis Joplin; Arlo Guthrie; Joe Cocker; Joan Baez; Crosby, Stills, Nash and Young; Creedence Clearwater Revival.
Record the personal recollections of a Woodstock participant.
Report on Yasgur's Farm: before and after.

## SUGGESTIONS FOR RELATED TOPICS

Life and career of a performing artist or group from the 1960s
Hippie culture
Woodstock II
Haight Ashbury, San Francisco

This RESEARCH TOPIC GUIDE is intended to help the library user find information and materials on a particular topic in many sources throughout the library. Resources on this topic are not limited to those described and availability will depend upon the individual library. Feel free to ask a librarian for assistance.

# IV

# Biography Research Topic Guides

# V. C. Andrews (194?–1986)

## BACKGROUND

Since her first novel, *Flowers in the Attic*, was published in 1979, V. C. Andrews has remained a popular writer of horror stories, especially among teenagers. Her tales of childhood terror, inhabited by cruel grandmothers, incest victims, and abused children, continue to fascinate readers years after her death.

## LOOK UNDER THE FOLLOWING SUBJECTS IN THE CATALOG (CARD OR COMPUTER)

Andrews, V. C. (Virginia C.)
Horror tales, American—History and criticism

## REFERENCE MATERIALS THAT MAY HELP (BOOKS OR CD-ROMS)

Garrett, Agnes, and Helga P. McCue, eds. *Authors and Artists for Young Adults*, Vol. 4, 1990.

Kies, Cosette. *Presenting Young Adult Horror Fiction*, 1992.

Locher, Frances C., ed. *Contemporary Authors*, Vols. 97–100, 1981.

Straub, Deborah A., ed. *Contemporary Authors New Revision Series*, Vol. 21, 1987.

## PERIODICAL INDEXES TO SEARCH (BOOKS OR CD-ROMS)

EBSCO Magazine Article Summaries
InfoTrac
Readers' Guide to Periodical Literature
WILSONDISC

## ONLINE DATABASES TO SEARCH

America Online
CompuServe
Dialog
Internet
Prodigy

## KEY WORDS AND DESCRIPTORS FOR PERIODICAL INDEX AND ONLINE SEARCHES

Andrews, V. C.

**VIDEOTAPE ON THIS TOPIC**

*Flowers in the Attic*. New World Video, 1988.

**FICTION BOOKS RELATING TO TOPIC**

Fiction section under Andrews, V. C.

**SUGGESTIONS FOR NARROWING THIS TOPIC**

Analyze a common theme in Andrews's writing; e.g., sexual abuse, incest, sin, cruelty.

Andrews's work could be classified in the gothic horror genre. Discuss her use of gothic horror literary techniques.

Comment on Andrews's use of personal memories in her work.

Write about one of Andrews's series; e.g., Dollanganger, Casteel, Cutler.

**SUGGESTIONS FOR RELATED TOPICS**

Charlotte Brontë

Daphne DuMaurier

Dean Koontz

Edgar Allan Poe

Stephen King

This RESEARCH TOPIC GUIDE is intended to help the library user find information and materials on a particular topic in many sources throughout the library. Resources on this topic are not limited to those described and availability will depend upon the individual library. Feel free to ask a librarian for assistance.

# Maya Angelou (1928– )

**BACKGROUND**

Maya Angelou, author, poet, storyteller, playwright, and performer is considered one of the great voices of African-American literature and experience. Her five autobiographies describe growing up black in the South. Her works reflect the humiliation and hardships of poverty and discrimination, as well as the dignity of those who survive it.

**BROWSE FOR BOOKS ON THE SHELF USING THESE CALL NUMBERS**

> Biography section under Angelou, Maya
>
> 811.54 Angelou

**LOOK UNDER THE FOLLOWING SUBJECTS IN THE CATALOG (CARD OR COMPUTER)**

> Angelou, Maya
>
> Angelou, Maya—Biography
>
> Afro-American women authors—20th century
>
> Afro-American women authors—20th century—Biography

**REFERENCE MATERIALS THAT MAY HELP (BOOKS OR CD-ROMS)**

> Beetz, Kirk H., ed. *Beacham's Guide to Literature for Young Adults*, Vol. 2, 1989.
>
> Collier, Laurie, ed. *Authors and Artists for Young Adults*, Vol. 7, 1991.
>
> Davis, Thadious M., and Trudier Harris, eds. *Dictionary of Literary Biography*, Vol. 38, 1985.
>
> Graham, Judith, ed. *Current Biography Yearbook, 1994.*
>
> Marowski, Daniel G., ed. *Contemporary Literary Criticism*, Vol. 35, 1985.

**PERIODICAL INDEXES TO SEARCH (BOOKS OR CD-ROMS)**

> Biography Index
>
> EBSCO Magazine Article Summaries
>
> InfoTrac
>
> Readers' Guide to Periodical Literature
>
> WILSONDISC

**ONLINE DATABASES TO SEARCH**

> America Online

CompuServe
Dialog
Internet
Prodigy

## KEY WORDS AND DESCRIPTORS FOR PERIODICAL INDEX AND ONLINE SEARCHES

Angelou, Maya

## VIDEOTAPES ON THIS TOPIC

*Maya Angelou*. Netche, 1982.
*Maya Angelou's America: A Journey of the Heart*. PBS Video, 1993.

## SUGGESTIONS FOR NARROWING THIS TOPIC

Critique "On the Pulse of Morning," a poem composed for President Clinton's inauguration.
Discuss the relationship of Angelou's life and work.
Relate the early life of Maya Angelou.

## SUGGESTIONS FOR RELATED TOPICS

Compare Maya Angelou with Toni Morrison, Alice Walker, Rita Dove, or Gloria Naylor; discuss aspects of their life and work.
Find and discuss examples of metaphor in the poetry of Maya Angelou.
How does Angelou's work express the African-American experience?

This RESEARCH TOPIC GUIDE is intended to help the library user find information and materials on a particular topic in many sources throughout the library. Resources on this topic are not limited to those described and availability will depend upon the individual library. Feel free to ask a librarian for assistance.

# Bob Dylan (1941– )

## BACKGROUND

Perhaps more than anyone else, Bob Dylan, in his music, lyrics, and attitude, represented the 1960s generation. Beginning with folk music and moving on to rock, he expressed the hope, frustration, and anger of his followers. The culture of the 1960s has become popular again and Bob Dylan has a following among today's teenagers.

## BROWSE FOR BOOKS ON THE SHELF USING THESE CALL NUMBERS

Biography section under Dylan, Bob

784.092

784.4–784.4924

## LOOK UNDER THE FOLLOWING SUBJECTS IN THE CATALOG (CARD OR COMPUTER)

Dylan, Bob

Rock music—United States—History and criticism

Musicians—Biography—Dictionaries

## REFERENCE MATERIALS THAT MAY HELP (BOOKS OR CD-ROMS)

Charters, Ann, ed. *Dictionary of Literary Biography*, Vol. 16, 1983.

Clarke, Donald. *Penguin Encyclopedia of Popular Music*, 1991.

Draper, James P., ed. *Contemporary Literary Criticism*, Vol. 77, 1993.

Hitchcock, H. Wiley, and Stanley Sadie, eds. *The New Grove Dictionary of American Music*, 1986.

Leblanc, Michael L. *Contemporary Musicians: Profiles of the People in Music*, 1994.

## PERIODICAL INDEXES TO SEARCH (BOOKS OR CD-ROMS)

Biography Index

EBSCO Magazine Article Summaries

InfoTrac

Readers' Guide to Periodical Literature

## ONLINE DATABASES TO SEARCH

America Online

CompuServe

Dialog

Internet

Prodigy

## KEY WORDS AND DESCRIPTORS FOR PERIODICAL INDEX AND ONLINE SEARCHES

Dylan, Bob

## VIDEOTAPE ON THIS TOPIC

*Bob Dylan: The 30th Anniversary Concert Celebration.* Columbia Music Video, 1993.

## SUGGESTIONS FOR NARROWING THIS TOPIC

Analyze or interpret lyrics from some of Dylan's work.

Choose a particular period of Dylan's work and comment; e.g., folk, electronic, Christian, rock.

Discuss Dylan's writings and drawings.

Discuss the influence of Dylan on music of the 1960s, 1970s, and beyond.

## SUGGESTIONS FOR RELATED TOPICS

Woodstock Music Festival

1960s culture

Joan Baez

Hippies and other counterculture groups

Traveling Wilburys

This RESEARCH TOPIC GUIDE is intended to help the library user find information and materials on a particular topic in many sources throughout the library. Resources on this topic are not limited to those described and availability will depend upon the individual library. Feel free to ask a librarian for assistance.

# Bill Gates (1956–   )

## BACKGROUND

Once a young computer hacker building computers in his garage, Bill Gates is now chief executive officer (CEO) of Microsoft Corporation, one of the world's most profitable companies. Bill Gates has captured our attention with his innovative management concepts, business acumen, and dynamic marketing promotions.

## BROWSE FOR BOOKS ON THE SHELF USING THESE CALL NUMBERS

Biography section under Gates, Bill
338.76–338.761

## LOOK UNDER THE FOLLOWING SUBJECTS IN THE CATALOG (CARD OR COMPUTER)

Gates, Bill
Microsoft Corporation—History
Computer software industry—United States—History

## REFERENCE MATERIALS THAT MAY HELP (BOOKS OR CD-ROMS)

*Biographies on File.* Facts on File, January 1996.
Moritz, Charles, ed. *Current Biography Yearbook, 1991.*
*Newsmakers: The People behind Today's Headlines.* Gale, 1993.

## PERIODICAL INDEXES TO SEARCH (BOOKS OR CD-ROMS)

Biography Index
Business NewsBank
EBSCO Magazine Article Summaries
InfoTrac
NewsBank and other newspaper indexes
Readers' Guide to Periodical Literature
WILSONDISC

## ONLINE DATABASES TO SEARCH

America Online
CompuServe
Dialog
Internet
Prodigy

## KEY WORDS AND DESCRIPTORS FOR PERIODICAL INDEX AND ONLINE SEARCHES

Gates, Bill
Gates, William H.
Microsoft Corporation
Windows (software program)

## NATIONAL ORGANIZATION TO CONTACT FOR ADDITIONAL INFORMATION

Microsoft Corporation, One Microsoft Way, Redmond, WA 98052–6399.

## SUGGESTIONS FOR NARROWING THIS TOPIC

Analyze the relationship between Microsoft and IBM.
Choose one or more of Microsoft's innovations and discuss their importance
    in the computer industry; e.g., MS-DOS, Windows.
Discuss the history of the Microsoft Corporation.
Discuss the role Bill Gates plays as CEO of Microsoft.

## SUGGESTIONS FOR RELATED TOPICS

Computer Crime
IBM
Information Highway/Internet
Steve Jobs
Relate the history of the computer software industry in the United States.

This RESEARCH TOPIC GUIDE is intended to help the library user find information and materials on a particular topic in many sources throughout the library. Resources on this topic are not limited to those described and availability will depend upon the individual library. Feel free to ask a librarian for assistance.

# Stephen Hawking (1942–  )

## BACKGROUND

Despite living with amyotrophic lateral sclerosis, a severe, crippling disease, Dr. Stephen Hawking, the world-famous British physicist, has developed complex theories on the origin and future of the universe, black holes, and other phenomena of the cosmos.

## BROWSE FOR BOOKS ON THE SHELF USING THESE CALL NUMBERS

Biography section under Hawking, Stephen

523.1

530.1

## LOOK UNDER THE FOLLOWING SUBJECT IN THE CATALOG (CARD OR COMPUTER)

Hawking, S. W. (Stephen W.)

## REFERENCE MATERIALS THAT MAY HELP (BOOKS OR CD-ROMS)

Hile, Kevin, and E. A. Deschenes, eds. *Authors and Artists for Young Adults*, Vol. 13, 1994.

Matuz, Roger, ed. *Contemporary Literary Criticism*, Vol. 63, 1991.

Moritz, Charles, ed. *Current Biography Yearbook, 1984.*

Trotzky, Susan, ed. *Contemporary Authors*, Vol. 129, 1990.

## PERIODICAL INDEXES TO SEARCH (BOOKS OR CD-ROMS)

Biography Index

EBSCO Magazine Article Summaries

InfoTrac

Readers' Guide to Periodical Literature

WILSONDISC

## ONLINE DATABASES TO SEARCH

America Online

CompuServe

Dialog

Internet

Prodigy

## KEY WORDS AND DESCRIPTORS FOR PERIODICAL INDEX AND ONLINE SEARCHES

Hawking, Stephen

## VIDEOTAPES ON THIS TOPIC

*A Brief History of Time*. Gordon Freedman Productions, 1992.
*Stephen Hawking: The Universe Within*. Cabisco Teleproductions, 1989.

## NATIONAL ORGANIZATION TO CONTACT FOR ADDITIONAL INFORMATION

Department of Applied Mathematics and Theoretical Physics, Cambridge University, Silver Street, Cambridge CB3 9EW, England.

## SUGGESTIONS FOR NARROWING THIS TOPIC

Comment on the relationship between science and religion in Hawking's philosophy.
Discuss the early life of Stephen Hawking and how it led to his professional success.
Discuss how Hawking copes with his physical limitations.
Examine Hawking's black hole theories.

## SUGGESTIONS FOR RELATED TOPICS

Amyotrophic lateral sclerosis (Lou Gehrig's disease)
Astrophysics
Cosmology
Quantum mechanics
Quarks

This RESEARCH TOPIC GUIDE is intended to help the library user find information and materials on a particular topic in many sources throughout the library. Resources on this topic are not limited to those described and availability will depend upon the individual library. Feel free to ask a librarian for assistance.

# Jimi Hendrix (1942–1970)

**BACKGROUND**

In his relatively short life Jimi Hendrix became a rock-and-roll icon, playing electric guitar and composing for his rock group, the Jimi Hendrix Experience. After his drug-related death in 1970, he became a legend and his influence and charisma endure.

**BROWSE FOR BOOKS ON THE SHELF USING THESE CALL NUMBERS**

> Biography section under Hendrix, Jimi
> 787.87

**LOOK UNDER THE FOLLOWING SUBJECTS IN THE CATALOG (CARD OR COMPUTER)**

> Hendrix, Jimi
> Jimi Hendrix Experience
> Rock musicians—United States—Biography
> Musicians—Biography—Dictionaries

**REFERENCE MATERIALS THAT MAY HELP (BOOKS OR CD-ROMS)**

> Clarke, Donald, ed. *The Penguin Encyclopedia of Popular Music*, 1989.
> Garraty, John A., and Mark C. Carnes, eds. *Dictionary of American Biography*, Supplement 8, 1988.
> Hitchcock, H. Wiley, and Stanley Sadie, ed. *The New Grove Dictionary of American Music*, 1986.
> LeBlance, Michael L. *Contemporary Musicians: Profiles of the People in Music*, 1994.

**PERIODICAL INDEXES TO SEARCH (BOOKS OR CD-ROMS)**

> Biography Index
> EBSCO Magazine Article Summaries
> InfoTrac
> Readers' Guide to Periodical Literature
> WILSONDISC

**ONLINE DATABASES TO SEARCH**

> America Online
> CompuServe
> Dialog
> Internet
> Prodigy

## KEY WORDS AND DESCRIPTORS FOR PERIODICAL INDEX AND ONLINE SEARCHES

Hendrix, Jimi

## VIDEOTAPES ON THIS TOPIC

*Jimi Hendrix*. Warner Home Video, 1989.
*Woodstock*. Warner Home Video, 1989.

## NATIONAL ORGANIZATION TO CONTACT FOR ADDITIONAL INFORMATION

Jimi Hendrix Information Management Institute, P.O. Box 374, Des Plains, IL 60016.

## SUGGESTIONS FOR NARROWING THIS TOPIC

Analyze the lyrics and poetry in the works of Hendrix.
Comment on the influence of Hendrix on rock music.
Describe the Jimi Hendrix Exhibition (traveling multimedia art show).
Discuss the Jimi Hendrix Experience and their contribution to rock music.

## SUGGESTIONS FOR RELATED TOPICS

Bob Dylan
Rolling Stones
Van Morrison
Woodstock (Musical) Festival

This RESEARCH TOPIC GUIDE is intended to help the library user find information and materials on a particular topic in many sources throughout the library. Resources on this topic are not limited to those described and availability will depend upon the individual library. Feel free to ask a librarian for assistance.

# S. E. Hinton (1950–  )

## BACKGROUND

After publishing *The Outsiders* at the age of seventeen, S. E. (Susan Eloise) Hinton went on to write four other realistic novels about teenagers and the serious problems they deal with such as abortion, drug abuse, death, and divorce. Her books continue to be popular among teenage readers.

## BROWSE FOR BOOKS ON THE SHELF USING THESE CALL NUMBERS

Biography section under Hinton, S. E.
813.54

## LOOK UNDER THE FOLLOWING SUBJECTS IN THE CATALOG (CARD OR COMPUTER)

Hinton, S. E.
Hinton, S. E.—Criticism and interpretation

## REFERENCE MATERIALS THAT MAY HELP (BOOKS OR CD-ROMS)

Commire, Anne, ed. *Something about the Author*, Vol. 58, 1990.
Donelson, Kenneth, and Aileen P. Nilsen. *Literature for Today's Young Adults*, 1993.
Garrett, Agnes, and Helga P. McCue, eds. *Authors and Artists for Young Adults*, Vol. 2, 1989.
Lesniak, James G., ed. *Contemporary Authors New Revision Series*, Vol. 32, 1991.
Stine, Jean C., and Daniel G. Marowski, eds. *Contemporary Literary Criticism*, Vol. 30, 1984.

## PERIODICAL INDEXES TO SEARCH (BOOKS OR CD-ROMS)

Biography Index
EBSCO Magazine Article Summaries
InfoTrac
Readers' Guide to Periodical Literature
WILSONDISC

## ONLINE DATABASES TO SEARCH

Dialog
Internet

## KEY WORDS AND DESCRIPTORS FOR PERIODICAL INDEX AND ONLINE SEARCHES

Hinton, S. E.

## VIDEOTAPES ON THIS TOPIC

The following books by Hinton have been made into movies and are available on videotape:

*The Outsiders*. Warner Home Video, 1983.

*Rumblefish*. Universal-MCA Home Video, 1983.

*Tex*. Walt Disney Home Video, 1982.

*That Was Then, This Is Now*. Paramount Home Video, 1985.

## FICTION BOOKS RELATING TO TOPIC

Fiction section under Hinton, S. E.

## SUGGESTIONS FOR NARROWING THIS TOPIC

Analyze the setting of one or more of Hinton's works and its impact on the characters.

Compare Hinton's books with the film adaptations.

Compare *Rumblefish* or *The Outsiders* with another young adult novel such as *The Chocolate War* or *Catcher in the Rye*.

## SUGGESTIONS FOR RELATED TOPICS

Child abuse

Discuss another author who writes adolescent-problem novels; e.g., Robert Cormier, Richard Peck, Chris Crutcher, Cynthia Vogt.

Teenage street gangs

Teenage violence

This RESEARCH TOPIC GUIDE is intended to help the library user find information and materials on a particular topic in many sources throughout the library. Resources on this topic are not limited to those described and availability will depend upon the individual library. Feel free to ask a librarian for assistance.

# Stephen King (1947–  )

**BACKGROUND**

A favorite author of many teenagers, Stephen King has written over twenty-five works of horror fiction under his own name and the pseudonym Richard Bachman. His unique combination of the macabre, black humor, psychic phenomena, and popular culture has great appeal in all formats: book, movie, and television.

**BROWSE FOR BOOKS ON THE SHELF USING THESE CALL NUMBERS**

> Biography section under King, Stephen
>
> 791.43–791.435
>
> 813.54

**LOOK UNDER THE FOLLOWING SUBJECTS IN THE CATALOG (CARD OR COMPUTER)**

> King, Stephen—Criticism and interpretation
>
> King, Stephen—Interviews
>
> Horror tales—History and criticism
>
> Horror films—History and criticism

**REFERENCE MATERIALS THAT MAY HELP (BOOKS OR CD-ROMS)**

> Garrett, Agnes, and Helga P. McCue, eds. *Authors and Artists for Young Adults*, Vol. 1, 1989.
>
> Kies, Cosette. *Presenting Young Adult Horror Fiction*, 1992.
>
> Lesniack, James G., ed. *Contemporary Authors New Revision Series*, Vol. 30, 1990.
>
> Marowski, Daniel G., ed. *Contemporary Literary Criticism*, Vol. 37, 1986.

**PERIODICAL INDEXES TO SEARCH (BOOKS OR CD-ROMS)**

> Biography Index
>
> EBSCO Magazine Article Summaries
>
> InfoTrac
>
> Readers' Guide to Periodical Literature
>
> WILSONDISC

**ONLINE DATABASES TO SEARCH**

> America Online
>
> CompuServe
>
> Dialog

Internet

Prodigy

## KEY WORDS AND DESCRIPTORS FOR PERIODICAL INDEX AND ONLINE SEARCHES

King, Stephen

Horror tales

Horror films

## VIDEOTAPES ON THIS TOPIC

Many of King's works are available on videotape.

*Stephen King's Golden Years*. Worldvision Home Video, 1991.

## FICTION BOOKS RELATING TO TOPIC

Fiction section under King, Stephen

## NATIONAL ORGANIZATION TO CONTACT FOR ADDITIONAL INFORMATION

Castle Rock, the Official Stephen King Newsletter, P.O. Box 8183, Bangor, ME 04401.

## SUGGESTIONS FOR NARROWING THIS TOPIC

Analyze repetitive themes in King's works: the outsider as hero, struggle between good and evil, coming of age.

Comment on King's use of humor.

Discuss King's use of commercial, or popular, culture in his works.

## SUGGESTIONS FOR RELATED TOPICS

Dean Koontz

Gothic horror novel literary genre

Popularity of horror fiction among teenagers

R. L. Stine

Tabitha King

This RESEARCH TOPIC GUIDE is intended to help the library user find information and materials on a particular topic in many sources throughout the library. Resources on this topic are not limited to those described and availability will depend upon the individual library. Feel free to ask a librarian for assistance.

# Madeleine L'Engle (1918– )

**BACKGROUND**

Madeleine L'Engle is a prolific writer of fiction, poetry, plays and nonfiction for both children and adults. Best known for her Time Fantasy series, she combines fantasy, science fiction and a cast of recurring characters that have captured the imagination of young adults and children for decades. Her essays and journals reflect her unusual childhood, family life and spiritual philosophy.

**BROWSE FOR BOOKS ON THE SHELF USING THESE CALL NUMBERS**

Biography section under L'Engle, Madeleine

**LOOK UNDER THE FOLLOWING SUBJECT IN THE CATALOG (CARD OR COMPUTER)**

L'Engle, Madeleine

**REFERENCE MATERIALS THAT MAY HELP (BOOKS OR CD-ROMS)**

Bryfonski, Dedria, ed. *Contemporary Literary Criticism*, Vol. 12, 1980.
Estes, Glenn E., ed. *Dictionary of Literary Biography*, Vol. 52, 1986.
Garrett, Agnes, and Helga P. McCue, eds. *Authors and Artists for Young Adults*, Vol. 1, 1989.
Trosky, Susan M., ed. *Contemporary Authors New Revision Series*, Vol. 39, 1992.

**PERIODICAL INDEXES TO SEARCH (BOOKS OR CD-ROMS)**

Biography Index
EBSCO Magazine Article Summaries
InfoTrac
Readers' Guide to Periodical Literature
WILSONDISC

**ONLINE DATABASES TO SEARCH**

Dialog
Internet

**KEY WORDS AND DESCRIPTORS FOR PERIODICAL INDEX AND ONLINE SEARCHES**

L'Engle, Madeleine

## FICTION BOOKS RELATING TO TOPIC

Fiction section under L'Engle, Madeleine

## SUGGESTIONS FOR NARROWING THIS TOPIC

Analyze the references to Christianity in the writings of L'Engle.
Discuss L'Engle's Time Fantasy series.
Read and interpret the poetry of L'Engle.
Research the life of Madeleine L'Engle and its impact on her work.

## SUGGESTIONS FOR RELATED TOPICS

Anne McCaffrey
C. S. Lewis
Ursula K. LeGuin

This RESEARCH TOPIC GUIDE is intended to help the library user find information and materials on a particular topic in many sources throughout the library. Resources on this topic are not limited to those described and availability will depend upon the individual library. Feel free to ask a librarian for assistance.

# John Lennon (1940–1980)

**BACKGROUND**

Lead member of the English rock group the Beatles, John Lennon was a talented artist, writer, poet, and musician. After the Beatles reached stardom and eventually disbanded, Lennon enjoyed continued artistic success with his wife and partner, Yoko Ono. In 1980 he was murdered by a gunman outside his New York City apartment building.

**BROWSE FOR BOOKS ON THE SHELF USING THESE CALL NUMBERS**

Biography section under Lennon, John
784.54–784.54009
784.09–784.3

**LOOK UNDER THE FOLLOWING SUBJECTS IN THE CATALOG (CARD OR COMPUTER)**

Lennon, John
Beatles
Rock musicians—Biography

**REFERENCE MATERIALS THAT MAY HELP (BOOKS OR CD-ROMS)**

Blake, Lord, and C. S. Nicholls, eds. *Dictionary of National Biography, 1971–1980*, 1986.
Clarke, Donald, ed. *The Penguin Encyclopedia of Popular Music*, 1989.
Locher, Frances C., ed. *Contemporary Authors*, Vol. 102, 1981.
Marowski, Daniel G., ed. *Contemporary Literary Criticism*, Vol. 35, 1985.
Moritz, Charles, ed. *Current Biography Yearbook, 1965*.
General encyclopedias

**PERIODICAL INDEXES TO SEARCH (BOOKS OR CD-ROMS)**

Biography Index
EBSCO Magazine Article Summaries
InfoTrac
Readers' Guide to Periodical Literature

**ONLINE DATABASES TO SEARCH**

America Online
CompuServe
Dialog
Internet
Prodigy

## KEY WORDS AND DESCRIPTORS FOR PERIODICAL INDEX AND ONLINE SEARCHES

Lennon, John
Ono, Yoko
Beatles

## VIDEOTAPES ON THIS TOPIC

*Imagine: John Lennon*. Capitol, 1988.
*John Lennon and Yoko Ono: The Bed-In*. Music, Inc., 1969.
*John Lennon Video Collection*. Capitol-EMI Music, 1992.
*Sergeant Pepper's Lonely Hearts Club Band*. MCA Home Video, 1990.
*Yellow Submarine*. MGM/VA Home Video, 1987.

## NATIONAL ORGANIZATIONS TO CONTACT FOR ADDITIONAL INFORMATION

Rock and Roll Hall of Fame, C/O Atlantic Records, 75 Rockefeller Plaza, 2nd Floor, New York, NY 10019.
Rock and Roll Hall of Fame and Museum, 1 Key Plaza, Cleveland, OH 44115.

## SUGGESTIONS FOR NARROWING THIS TOPIC

Analyze the lyrics of Lennon's music.
Discuss John Lennon as a social activist.
Discuss the significance of Lennon's drawings.
Comment on the influence of Lennon's music on the 1960s and 1970s music scene.
How did Lennon's early life affect his career?

## SUGGESTIONS FOR RELATED TOPICS

"British Invasion" of rock musicians during the 1960s
George Harrison
Julian Lennon
Paul McCartney
Ringo Starr
Yoko Ono

This RESEARCH TOPIC GUIDE is intended to help the library user find information and materials on a particular topic in many sources throughout the library. Resources on this topic are not limited to those described and availability will depend upon the individual library. Feel free to ask a librarian for assistance.

# Andrew Lloyd Webber (1948–   )

## BACKGROUND

Famed British composer of musicals Andrew Lloyd Webber's genius lies in combining enduring motifs from literature, religion, and history with themes from current popular culture. The music, staging, and storylines of *Evita*, *Phantom of the Opera*, *Cats*, and numerous other musicals prove popular with audiences and critics.

## BROWSE FOR BOOKS ON THE SHELF USING THESE CALL NUMBERS

Biography section under Lloyd Webber, Andrew
780.78–782.8

## LOOK UNDER THE FOLLOWING SUBJECTS IN THE CATALOG (CARD OR COMPUTER)

Lloyd Webber, Andrew
   (occasionally found under Webber, Andrew Lloyd)

## REFERENCE MATERIALS THAT MAY HELP (BOOKS OR CD-ROMS)

Commire, Anne, ed. *Something about the Author*, Vol. 56, 1989.

Gareffa, Peter M., ed. *Newsmakers: The People behind Today's Headlines*, 1989.

Garrett, Agnes, and Helga P. McCue, eds. *Authors and Artists for Young Adults*, Vol. 1, 1989.

LaBlance, Michael L., ed. *Contemporary Musicians: Profiles of the People in Music*, 1994.

May, Hal, ed. *Contemporary Authors*, Vol. 116, 1986.

Rooney, Terrie M., ed. *Contemporary Theater, Film and Television*, 1995.

## PERIODICAL INDEXES TO SEARCH (BOOKS OR CD-ROMS)

Biography Index
EBSCO Magazine Article Summaries
InfoTrac
Readers' Guide to Periodical Literature
WILSONDISC

## ONLINE DATABASES TO SEARCH

America Online
CompuServe
Dialog

Internet
Prodigy

## KEY WORDS AND DESCRIPTORS FOR PERIODICAL INDEX AND ONLINE SEARCHES

Lloyd Webber, Andrew
Broadway musicals
Broadway shows
Use titles of specific productions; e.g., *Evita, Sunset Boulevard, Phantom of the Opera.*

## VIDEOTAPES ON THIS TOPIC

*Andrew Lloyd Webber: The Premier Collection.* PolyGram Video, 1992.
*Requiem.* Kultur, 1985.

## FICTION BOOKS RELATING TO TOPIC

Bischoff, David. *Phantom of the Opera*, 1976.
Leroux, Gaston. *Phantom of the Opera*, 1938.

## SUGGESTIONS FOR NARROWING THIS TOPIC

Choose one or more works to analyze; e.g., *Jesus Christ Superstar, Cats, Evita.*
Compare one of Lloyd Webber's musicals with the original work; e.g., *Cats* and T. S. Eliot's *Old Possum's Book of Practical Cats.*
Discuss why *Cats* is one of the longest-running musicals ever to appear on Broadway.

## SUGGESTIONS FOR RELATED TOPICS

History of Broadway musicals
Set design
Staging of musicals
Stephen Sondheim

This RESEARCH TOPIC GUIDE is intended to help the library user find information and materials on a particular topic in many sources throughout the library. Resources on this topic are not limited to those described and availability will depend upon the individual library. Feel free to ask a librarian for assistance.

# Toni Morrison (1931- )

## BACKGROUND

A Pulitzer Prize–winning author, Toni Morrison writes about the black experience in America from the viewpoint of her unforgettable characters. Her works focus on a range of issues, including slavery, discrimination, relationships between blacks and whites, and women. Morrison brings a sense of the supernatural to her writing and a respect for her ancient heritage.

## BROWSE FOR BOOKS ON THE SHELF USING THESE CALL NUMBERS

Biography section under Morrison, Toni
813
813.54

## LOOK UNDER THE FOLLOWING SUBJECTS IN THE CATALOG (CARD OR COMPUTER)

Afro-American women novelists—20th century
American fiction—Women authors—History and criticism

## REFERENCE MATERIALS THAT MAY HELP (BOOKS OR CD-ROMS)

Draper, James P., ed. *Contemporary Literary Criticism*, Vol. 81, 1994.
Garrett, Agnes, and Helga P. McCue, eds. *Authors and Artists for Young Adults*, Vol. 1, 1989.
Giles, James R., ed. *Dictionary of Literary Biography*, Vol. 143, 1994.
Kranz, Rachel E. *The Biographical Dictionary of Black Americans*, 1992.

## PERIODICAL INDEXES TO SEARCH (BOOKS OR CD-ROMS)

Biography Index
EBSCO Magazine Article Summaries
InfoTrac
Readers' Guide to Periodical Literature
WILSONDISC

## ONLINE DATABASES TO SEARCH

America Online
Biography Index
CompuServe
Dialog
Internet
Prodigy

## KEY WORDS AND DESCRIPTORS FOR PERIODICAL INDEX AND ONLINE SEARCHES

Morrison, Toni

## VIDEOTAPES ON THIS TOPIC

*Toni Morrison.* Home Vision, 1987.

*Toni Morrison: A Conversation with Toni Morrison.* California Newsreel, 1992.

## FICTION BOOKS RELATING TO TOPIC

Fiction section under Morrison, Toni

## SUGGESTIONS FOR NARROWING THIS TOPIC

Choose a particular work to analyze; e.g., *Beloved, The Bluest Eye, Tar Baby.*

Comment on the impact of Morrison's early life on her work.

Compare Morrison with another African-American woman writer; e.g., Alice Walker.

Discuss Morrison's views on racism, black women, or growing up in the South.

## SUGGESTIONS FOR RELATED TOPICS

Alice Walker

Maya Angelou

Rita Dove

This RESEARCH TOPIC GUIDE is intended to help the library user find information and materials on a particular topic in many sources throughout the library. Resources on this topic are not limited to those described and availability will depend upon the individual library. Feel free to ask a librarian for assistance.

# Nostradamus (1503-1566)

**BACKGROUND**

Still popular after 400 years, the French prophet Nostradamus published many books of poems, prophecies, and translations during his life. Now, at the end of the twentieth century, his predictions, influence, and reputation are being resurrected.

**BROWSE FOR BOOKS ON THE SHELF USING THIS CALL NUMBER**

133.32

**LOOK UNDER THE FOLLOWING SUBJECTS IN THE CATALOG (CARD OR COMPUTER)**

Nostradamus
Twentieth century—Forecasts
Prophecies
End of the world
Prophecies (Occultism)

**REFERENCE MATERIALS THAT MAY HELP (BOOKS OR CD-ROMS)**

Guiley, Rosemary Ellen. *Harper's Encyclopedia of Mystical and Paranormal Experience*, 1991.

*Mysteries of Mind, Space and Time: The Unexplained*. H. S. Stuttman, 1992.

Shaw, Eva. *Divining the Future: Prognostication from Astrology to Zoomancy*, 1995.

Shepard, Leslie A., ed. *Encyclopedia of Occultism and Parapsychology*, 1984.

General encyclopedias

**PERIODICAL INDEXES TO SEARCH (BOOKS OR CD-ROMS)**

EBSCO Magazine Article Summaries
InfoTrac
Readers' Guide to Periodical Literature
WILSONDISC

**ONLINE DATABASES TO SEARCH**

America Online
CompuServe
Dialog
Internet
Prodigy

## KEY WORDS AND DESCRIPTORS FOR PERIODICAL INDEX AND ONLINE SEARCHES

Nostradamus

Prophecies

## VIDEOTAPES ON THIS TOPIC

*Nostradamus*. American Video, 1988.

*The Man Who Saw Tomorrow*. Warner Home Video, 1990.

## FICTION BOOKS RELATING TO TOPIC

Asimov, Isaac. *Forward the Foundation,* 1993.

Dexter, Catherine. *The Oracle Doll*, 1985.

## SUGGESTIONS FOR NARROWING THIS TOPIC

Compare the writings of Nostradamus to the actual events he predicted.

Discuss the role of imagination, coincidence, and charisma in the success of Nostradamus.

Research the life and times of Nostradamus.

## SUGGESTIONS FOR RELATED TOPICS

Astrology

Fortune telling

Modern prophets; e.g., Edgar Cayce, Jeane Dixon, H. G. Welles

Religious prophets; e.g., Joseph Smith, Muhammad, Oracle of Delphi

This RESEARCH TOPIC GUIDE is intended to help the library user find information and materials on a particular topic in many sources throughout the library. Resources on this topic are not limited to those described and will depend upon the individual library. Feel free to ask a librarian for assistance.

# Georgia O'Keeffe (1887–1986)

**BACKGROUND**

Artist Georgia O'Keeffe's canvases seem larger than life. Her early New York skylines, the huge closeups of flowers, and desert scenes of bleached skulls and bones are representative of distinct periods in her art. O'Keeffe enjoyed an unconventional life with her husband, the photographer Alfred Stieglitz, and a literary and artistic circle of friends.

**BROWSE FOR BOOKS ON THE SHELF USING THESE CALL NUMBERS**

> Biography section under O'Keeffe, Georgia
> 759.13

**LOOK UNDER THE FOLLOWING SUBJECTS IN THE CATALOG (CARD OR COMPUTER)**

> O'Keeffe, Georgia
> Stieglitz, Alfred
> Art, Modern—20th century

**REFERENCE MATERIALS THAT MAY HELP (BOOKS OR CD-ROMS)**

> Chanticleer, Press, ed. *The Encyclopedia of American Art*, 1981.
> Janson, H. W., ed. *The History of Art*, 1986.
> Moritz, Charles, ed. *Current Biography Yearbook, 1964.*
> Osborne, Harold, ed. *The Oxford Companion to Twentieth Century Art*, 1981.
> General encyclopedias

**PERIODICAL INDEXES TO SEARCH (BOOKS OR CD-ROMS)**

> Biography Index
> EBSCO Magazine Article Summaries
> InfoTrac
> Readers' Guide to Periodical Literature
> WILSONDISC

**ONLINE DATABASES TO SEARCH**

> America Online
> CompuServe
> Dialog
> Internet
> Prodigy

**KEY WORDS AND DESCRIPTORS FOR PERIODICAL INDEX AND ONLINE SEARCHES**

O'Keeffe, Georgia

**VIDEOTAPES ON THIS TOPIC**

*Art and Life of Georgia O'Keeffe*. Educational Dimensions, 1989.
*Georgia O'Keeffe*. Home Vision, 1989.

**NATIONAL ORGANIZATIONS TO CONTACT FOR ADDITIONAL INFORMATION**

Art Institute of Chicago (Library or Shop), 111 S. Michigan Ave., Chicago, IL 60603–9947.
Metropolitan Museum of Art Bookshop, 5th Ave. and 82nd St., New York, NY 10028.
Museum of Modern Art Shop, 37 W. 53rd St., New York, NY 10019.

**SUGGESTIONS FOR NARROWING THIS TOPIC**

Choose a particular period or theme to discuss; e.g., flower paintings, desert scenes.
Describe the relationship between O'Keeffe and Stieglitz.
Relate the early life of Georgia O'Keeffe.
What did O'Keeffe reveal about herself and her art in her correspondence?

**SUGGESTIONS FOR RELATED TOPICS**

Alfred Stieglitz
Alice Neel
Faith Ringgold
Flowers as a theme in art
Frida Kahlo
Women artists in the 1920s and 1930s

This RESEARCH TOPIC GUIDE is intended to help the library user find information and materials on a particular topic in many sources throughout the library. Resources on this topic are not limited to those described and availability will depend upon the individual library. Feel free to ask a librarian for assistance.

# Dr. Seuss (Theodor Geisel, 1904–1991)

## BACKGROUND

Theodor Geisel, better known as Dr. Seuss and one of the best-loved authors and illustrators of childrens' books died in 1991. His work continues to be tremendously popular among all ages. His works can be understood on many levels with themes including self-confidence, discrimination, and responsibility.

## BROWSE FOR BOOKS ON THE SHELF USING THESE CALL NUMBERS

Biography section under Seuss, Dr.

## LOOK UNDER THE FOLLOWING SUBJECT IN THE CATALOG (CARD OR COMPUTER)

Seuss, Dr.

## REFERENCE MATERIALS THAT MAY HELP (BOOKS OR CD-ROMS)

Estes, Glenn E., ed. *Dictionary of Literary Biography*, Vol. 61, 1987.

Lystad, Mary H. *From Dr. Mather to Dr. Seuss*, 1980.

Moritz, Charles, ed. *Current Biography Yearbook, 1968.*

Smith, James Steel. *A Critical Approach to Children's Literature*, 1967.

Sutherland, Zena. *Children and Books*, 1986.

Telgen, Diane, ed. *Something about the Author*, Vol. 75, 1994. (and other vols.)

## PERIODICAL INDEXES TO SEARCH (BOOKS OR CD-ROMS)

Biography Index

EBSCO Magazine Article Summaries

InfoTrac

Readers' Guide to Periodical Literature

WILSONDISC

## ONLINE DATABASES TO SEARCH

America Online

CompuServe

Dialog

Internet

Prodigy

## KEY WORDS AND DESCRIPTORS FOR PERIODICAL INDEX AND ONLINE SEARCHES

Geisel, Theodor
Seuss, Dr.

## VIDEOTAPES ON THIS TOPIC

Many works by Dr. Seuss have been made into movies and are available on videotape.

## FICTION BOOKS RELATING TO TOPIC

Fiction section under Seuss, Dr.
Most works by Seuss will be found in the children's section of the library.

## NATIONAL ORGANIZATIONS TO CONTACT FOR ADDITIONAL INFORMATION

American Library Association, 50 E. Huron St., Chicago, IL 60611.
Children's Literature Association, P.O. Box 138, Battle Creek, MI 49016.

## SUGGESTIONS FOR NARROWING THIS TOPIC

Choose one of the following literary techniques to analyze in works by Seuss: rhythm and rhyme, satire, symbolism.
Discuss how Seuss used his writing to comment on social issues.
*Oh, the Places You'll Go!* spent many weeks on the *New York Times* Best Sellers List. Discuss possible reasons for this.

## SUGGESTIONS FOR RELATED TOPICS

Choose your favorite author of children's books to write about; e.g., Chris Van Allsburg, E. B. White.
Fairy tales
Use of symbolism in children's literature

This RESEARCH TOPIC GUIDE is intended to help the library user find information and materials on a particular topic in many sources throughout the library. Resources on this topic are not limited to those described and availability will depend upon the individual library. Feel free to ask a librarian for assistance.

# J.R.R. Tolkien (John Ronald Reuel, 1892–1973)

## BACKGROUND

English fantasy writer J.R.R. Tolkien wrote about Middle Earth and the mythical creatures who inhabited that fictional land. His works have become science fiction cult classics and, despite some controversy and criticism, remain favorites of children and adults.

## BROWSE FOR BOOKS ON THE SHELF USING THESE CALL NUMBERS

> Biography section under Tolkien, J.R.R.
> 823.912
> 828.912

## LOOK UNDER THE FOLLOWING SUBJECTS IN THE CATALOG (CARD OR COMPUTER)

> Tolkien, J.R.R.
> Fantastic fiction, English
> Middle Earth (Imaginary place)

## REFERENCE MATERIALS THAT MAY HELP (BOOKS OR CD-ROMS)

> Beetz, Kirk H., ed. *Beacham's Guide to Literature for Young Adults*, Vol. 5, 1991.
> Hile, Kevin, ed. *Authors and Artists for Young Adults*, Vol. 10, 1993.
> Lesniak, James G., ed. *Contemporary Authors New Revision Series*, Vol. 36, 1992.
> Oldsey, Bernard, ed. *Dictionary of Literary Biography*, 1983.
> Stade, George, ed. *British Writers, Supplement II*, 1992.

## PERIODICAL INDEXES TO SEARCH (BOOKS OR CD-ROMS)

> Biography Index
> EBSCO Magazine Article Summaries
> InfoTrac
> Readers' Guide to Periodical Literature
> WILSONDISC

## ONLINE DATABASES TO SEARCH

> America Online
> CompuServe
> Dialog
> Internet

Prodigy

## KEY WORDS AND DESCRIPTORS FOR PERIODICAL INDEX AND ONLINE SEARCHES

Tolkien, J.R.R.
Hobbit
Middle Earth
Lord of the Rings

## VIDEOTAPES ON THIS TOPIC

Many of Tolkien's works are available on videotapes.

## FICTION BOOKS RELATING TO TOPIC

Fiction section under Tolkien, J.R.R.

## NATIONAL ORGANIZATIONS TO CONTACT FOR ADDITIONAL INFORMATION

American Tolkien Society, C/O Phil Helms, P.O. Box 373, Highland, MI 48357–0373.
American Hobbit Association, Rivendell, EA 730-F, Northland Rd., Forest Park, OH 45240.
Elvish Linguistic Fellowship, 2509 Ambling Circle, Crofton, MD 21114.

## SUGGESTIONS FOR NARROWING THIS TOPIC

Choose one or more Tolkien characters to discuss.
Compare the *Lord of the Rings* computer game with Tolkien's work.
Describe Middle Earth, the fantasy land that serves as the setting for many Tolkien works.
Did Tolkien use his Lord of the Rings trilogy as a vehicle for his political philosophies?
Discuss Christian symbolism in *Lord of the Rings*.

## SUGGESTIONS FOR RELATED TOPICS

C. S. Lewis
Elves and trolls in literature
Fairy tales
Use of symbolism in fantasy literature

This RESEARCH TOPIC GUIDE is intended to help the library user find information and materials on a particular topic in many sources throughout the library. Resources on this topic are not limited to those described and availability will depend upon the individual library. Feel free to ask a librarian for assistance.

# Sojourner Truth (1797?-1883)

**BACKGROUND**

Black woman, orator, and former slave, Sojourner Truth traveled throughout the Midwest and New England in the late nineteenth century, speaking out against slavery and working to improve living conditions of black people in the United States.

**BROWSE FOR BOOKS ON THE SHELF USING THESE CALL NUMBERS**

Biography section under Truth, Sojourner
305.4209

**LOOK UNDER THE FOLLOWING SUBJECTS IN THE CATALOG (CARD OR COMPUTER)**

Truth, Sojourner
Afro-American abolitionists—Biography
Abolitionists—United States—Biography
Abolitionists

**REFERENCE MATERIALS THAT MAY HELP (BOOKS OR CD-ROMS)**

Hine, Charlene, et al., eds. *Black Women in America: An Historical Encyclopedia*, 1993.
Kranz, Rachel. *The Biographical Dictionary of Black Americans*, 1992.
Ploski, Harry A., and James Williams. *The Negro Encyclopedia: A Reference Work on the African American*, 1989.
Williams, Michael W., ed. *The African American Encyclopedia*, 1993.
General encyclopedias

**PERIODICAL INDEXES TO SEARCH (BOOKS OR CD-ROMS)**

Biography Index
EBSCO Magazine Article Summaries
InfoTrac
Readers' Guide to Periodical Literature
WILSONDISC

**ONLINE DATABASES TO SEARCH**

Dialog
Internet

## KEY WORDS AND DESCRIPTORS FOR PERIODICAL INDEX AND ONLINE SEARCHES

Truth, Sojourner
Abolition movement
Abolitionists

## VIDEOTAPE ON THIS TOPIC

*Sojourner Truth.* Schlessinger Video Productions, 1992.

## SUGGESTIONS FOR NARROWING THIS TOPIC

Analyze the religious transformation of Sojourner Truth.
Discuss the oratorical skills of Sojourner Truth.
Examine Sojourner Truth as an early feminist.
Investigate Sojourner Truth's friendship with other well-known abolitionists.

## SUGGESTIONS FOR RELATED TOPICS

Abolition Movement
Research another abolitionist; e.g., John Brown, Frederick Douglass, Harriet
    Jacobs, Lucretia Mott, Harriet Beecher Stowe, Harriet Tubman.
Underground Railroad

This RESEARCH TOPIC GUIDE is intended to help the library user find information and materials on a particular topic in many sources throughout the library. Resources on this topic are not limited to those described and availability will depend upon the individual library. Feel free to ask a librarian for assistance.

# Andy Warhol (1928–1987)

**BACKGROUND**

A leader of the pop art movement, Andy Warhol rose to fame in 1962 with his paintings of Campbell's soup cans. Controversial in life as well as death, Warhol's art, personality, and importance continue to be discussed.

**BROWSE FOR BOOKS ON THE SHELF USING THESE CALL NUMBERS**

> Biography section under Warhol, Andy
> 759.1
> 709–709.2
> 769.92

**LOOK UNDER THE FOLLOWING SUBJECTS IN THE CATALOG (CARD OR COMPUTER)**

> Warhol, Andy
> Pop art—United States
> Art, Modern—20th century

**REFERENCE MATERIALS THAT MAY HELP (BOOKS OR CD-ROMS)**

> Gunton, Sharon R., ed. *Contemporary Literary Criticism*, Vol. 20, 1982.
> Hile, Kevin. *Authors and Artists for Young Adults*, Vol. 12, 1994.
> Huyghe, Rene, ed. *Larousse Encyclopedia of Modern Art, from 1800 to the Present Day*, 1961.
> Kultermann, Udo. *New Realism*, 1972.
> Moritz, Charles, ed. *Current Biography Yearbook, 1986*.

**PERIODICAL INDEXES TO SEARCH (BOOKS OR CD-ROMS)**

> Biography Index
> EBSCO Magazine Article Summaries
> InfoTrac
> Readers' Guide to Periodical Literature
> WILSONDISC

**ONLINE DATABASES TO SEARCH**

> America Online
> CompuServe
> Dialog
> Internet

Prodigy

## KEY WORDS AND DESCRIPTORS FOR PERIODICAL INDEX AND ONLINE SEARCHES

Warhol, Andy
Pop art

## VIDEOTAPE ON THIS TOPIC

*Andy Warhol*. Home Vision, 1987.

## NATIONAL ORGANIZATION TO CONTACT FOR ADDITIONAL INFORMATION

Andy Warhol Museum, 117 Sandusky Street, Pittsburgh, PA 15212.

## SUGGESTIONS FOR NARROWING THIS TOPIC

Describe the underground culture of "The Factory."
Discuss the films made by Warhol. How do they relate to his art?
Relate the early life of Andy Warhol and its impact on his art.
Why is Warhol's work considered pop art?

## SUGGESTIONS FOR RELATED TOPICS

Pop art movement
Roy Lichtenstein
Ultra Violet, underground film star

This RESEARCH TOPIC GUIDE is intended to help the library user find information and materials on a particular topic in many sources throughout the library. Resources on this topic are not limited to those described and availability will depend upon the individual library. Feel free to ask a librarian for assistance.

# Ryan White (1972-1990)

## BACKGROUND

Ryan White became a hero to many and a model of courage and inspiration to young AIDS patients during his valiant struggle against the disease which finally took his life in April 1990. White, a hemophiliac, contracted AIDS from a blood transfusion and was subsequently barred from attending school in Kokomo, Indiana. He and his mother, Jeanne, sued the school system and won.

## BROWSE FOR BOOKS ON THE SHELF USING THESE CALL NUMBERS

Biography section under White, Ryan

## LOOK UNDER THE FOLLOWING SUBJECTS IN THE CATALOG (CARD OR COMPUTER)

White, Ryan
AIDS (Disease)—Patients

## REFERENCE BOOKS THAT MAY HELP (BOOKS OR CD-ROMS)

*Facts on File*
*Newsmakers: The People behind Today's Headlines*. Gale, 1990.

## PERIODICAL INDEXES TO SEARCH (BOOKS OR CD-ROMS)

EBSCO Magazine Article Summaries
InfoTrac
NewsBank and other newspaper indexes
Readers' Guide to Periodical Literature
WILSONDISC

## ONLINE DATABASES TO SEARCH

Internet
Dialog

## KEY WORDS AND DESCRIPTORS FOR PERIODICAL INDEX AND ONLINE SEARCHES

White, Ryan

## VIDEOTAPE ON THIS TOPIC

*Understanding AIDS: What Teens Need to Know*. Sunburst Communications, 1988.

## NATIONAL ORGANIZATION TO CONTACT FOR ADDITIONAL INFORMATION

Ryan White National Teen Education Program, C/O Athletes and Entertainers for Kids, P.O. Box 191, Bldg. G, Gardena, CA 90248–0191.

## SUGGESTIONS FOR NARROWING THIS TOPIC

Discuss Ryan White's celebrity friendships with Elton John, Michael Jackson, Phil Donahue, Greg Louganis, and others.

Discuss Ryan White's impact on public awareness of the AIDS crisis.

Investigate Ryan White's attempts to remain in school after his diagnosis.

Why is Ryan White considered a hero?

## SUGGESTIONS FOR RELATED TOPICS

AIDS in children

AIDS babies

Hemophilia

Ryan White Comprehensive AIDS Resources Emergency Act of 1992.

This RESEARCH TOPIC GUIDE is intended to help the library user find information and materials on a particular topic in many sources throughout the library. Resources on this topic are not limited to those described and availability will depend upon the individual library. Feel free to ask a librarian for assistance.

# Laura Ingalls Wilder (1867–1957)

**BACKGROUND**

Famous for her Little House stories, Laura Ingalls Wilder spent her childhood during the westward expansion movement, resettling frequently from log cabin, to prairie home, to sod house following her restless father and resourceful mother. She wrote in story, letter, and diary of her life and adventures as she journeyed westward.

**BROWSE FOR BOOKS ON THE SHELF USING THESE CALL NUMBERS**

> Biography section under Wilder, Laura Ingalls

**LOOK UNDER THE FOLLOWING SUBJECTS IN THE CATALOG (CARD OR COMPUTER)**

> Wilder, Laura Ingalls—1867–1957—Biography
> Wilder, Laura Ingalls—1867–1957—Criticism

**REFERENCE BOOKS THAT MAY HELP (BOOKS OR CD-ROMS)**

> Beetz, Kirk H., and Suzanne Niemeyer, eds. *Beacham's Guide to Literature for Young Adults*, Vol. 2, 1989.
> Cech, John, ed. *Dictionary of Literary Biography*, Vol. 22, 1983.
> Riley, Carolyn, and Barbara Harte, eds. *Contemporary Literary Criticism*, Vol. 2, 1974.
> Rothe, Anna, ed. *Current Biography Yearbook, 1948*.

**PERIODICAL INDEXES TO SEARCH (BOOKS OR CD-ROMS)**

> Biography Index
> EBSCO Magazine Article Summaries
> InfoTrac
> Readers' Guide to Periodical Literature
> WILSONDISC

**ONLINE DATABASES TO SEARCH**

> Dialog
> Internet

**KEY WORDS AND DESCRIPTORS FOR PERIODICAL INDEX AND ONLINE SEARCHES**

> Wilder, Laura Ingalls
> Ingalls, Charles
> Walnut Grove, MN

Pepin, WI
DeSmet, SD

## VIDEOTAPES ON THIS TOPIC

Laura Ingalls Wilder's Little House series (from the television series) is available on videotape.

## FICTION BOOKS RELATING TO TOPIC

Fiction section under Wilder, Laura Ingalls

MacBride, Roger Lea. *Little Farm in the Ozarks*, 1994.

————. *Little House on Rocky Ridge*, 1993.

## NATIONAL ORGANIZATION TO CONTACT FOR ADDITIONAL INFORMATION

Laura Ingalls Wilder Memorial Society, P.O. Box 269, Pepin, WI 54759.

## SUGGESTIONS FOR NARROWING THIS TOPIC

Compare and contrast the various homes and living arrangements described in the Little House series.

Compare the television version of Wilder's life with her own stories.

Describe food and cooking in the Ingalls home.

Examine customs of frontier America as portrayed in the writings of Laura Ingalls Wilder.

## SUGGESTIONS FOR RELATED TOPICS

Almanzo Wilder, Laura's husband

A favorite writer of children's books

History of the Conestoga wagon

Journalist Rose Lane Wilder, Laura's daughter

Pioneer women

This RESEARCH TOPIC GUIDE is intended to help the library user find information and materials on a particular topic in many sources throughout the library. Resources on this topic are not limited to those described and availability will depend upon the individual library. Feel free to ask a librarian for assistance.

# Malcolm X (1925-1965)

## BACKGROUND

Dynamic and charismatic leader of the Black Muslim movement, Malcolm X (born Malcolm Little) spent much of his career speaking out against the white culture and promoting black power and separation. Although he was murdered in 1965, Malcolm X's writings and political philosophy are influential today.

## BROWSE FOR BOOKS ON THE SHELF USING THESE CALL NUMBERS

Biography section under X, Malcolm
320.54–320.5409

## LOOK UNDER THE FOLLOWING SUBJECTS IN THE CATALOG (CARD OR COMPUTER)

X, Malcolm
Black Muslims—Biography
Afro-Americans—Biography

## REFERENCE BOOKS THAT MAY HELP (BOOKS OR CD-ROMS)

*CQ Researcher*, April 30, 1993.
Garraty, John A., ed. *Dictionary of American Biography: Supplement Seven, 1961–1965*, 1981.
Ploski, Harry A., and James Williams, eds. *The Negro Almanac: A Reference Work on the African American*, 1989.
Smythe, Mabel M. *The Black American Reference Book*, 1972.
General encyclopedias

## PERIODICAL INDEXES TO SEARCH (BOOKS OR CD-ROMS)

Biography Index
EBSCO Magazine Article Summaries
InfoTrac
NewsBank and other newspaper indexes
Readers' Guide to Periodical Literature
WILSONDISC

## ONLINE DATABASES TO SEARCH

America Online
CompuServe
Dialog
Internet

Prodigy

## KEY WORDS AND DESCRIPTORS FOR PERIODICAL INDEX AND ONLINE SEARCHES

X, Malcolm
Black Muslims
Black power

## VIDEOTAPES ON THIS TOPIC

*Malcolm X*. Warner Home Video, 1992.
*The Real Malcolm X: An Intimate Portrait of the Man*. CBS News–Fox Video, 1992.

## SUGGESTIONS FOR NARROWING THIS TOPIC

Comment on the assassination of Malcolm X and possible reasons for it.
Compare the philosophies of Malcolm X and Martin Luther King, Jr.
Critique one of Malcolm X's speeches.
Discuss the influence of Malcolm X in his own time; in our time.
Discuss the philosophy of Malcolm X (his ideas changed radically several times during his life).
Why has there been a resurgence of interest in Malcolm X in the 1990s?

## SUGGESTIONS FOR RELATED TOPICS

Black Muslim movement
Black nationalism
Black Panthers
Civil rights movement
Racism
Louis Farakhan
Martin Luther King, Jr.

This RESEARCH TOPIC GUIDE is intended to help the library user find information and materials on a particular topic in many sources throughout the library. Resources on this topic are not limited to those described and availability will depend upon the individual library. Feel free to ask a librarian for assistance.

# Appendixes

# Appendix A: Guide to Note-Taking Procedures

A thorough research paper depends on good note taking. Gather information pertinent to your research topic from many sources throughout the library. Use reference books, magazine and newspaper indexes, vertical (pamphlet) files, reference materials on CD-ROM or online databases, videotapes, and anything else that will provide you with knowledge in any format. Before taking any notes, read the information you have found to decide if it will be valuable for your research and will support your topic. Then follow these steps for successful note taking:

1. Use note cards to record the information you discover. (3" x 5" or whatever you prefer or your teacher requires).

2. Include the following on each note card:

*Heading*: the specific topic the note refers to.

*Note with one main idea*: this could be a fact, idea, statistic, opinion of an author or authority, or definition of a term.

*Bibliographic reference*: author (or title if there is no author) and page number of the source where information was obtained. If material came from an online database, such as America Online, Prodigy, or the Internet, indicate name of database.

*Your own opinion (optional)*: when appropriate, add your own opinion or comments in a special area of the card or in a different color ink to keep it separate from the author's opinion.

3. Use one of the following types of notes on each card:

*Paraphrase*: use your own words to express the idea or opinion of the author. Do not copy any information word for word because it will be more difficult to translate it into your own words later, when you are ready to write your report.

*Direct quotation*: use the author's exact words, enclosed in quotation marks, when they are particularly insightful or expressive or when you wish to attribute a particular statement to an author. Do not include direct quotations too often, as it is usually better to use your own words and thoughts in a research paper. Remember, you will give credit for the quotation in your paper using a footnote or internal documentation.

*Summary*: use your own words to note the main idea of a paragraph, page, or section of a reference source. Summarize when you want to include the general idea of a large amount of information.

Good note taking requires a balance between gathering enough information to write a complete report and recording it concisely and accurately on note cards. Following the steps presented here will help you achieve that goal.

# Appendix B: Guide to Bibliographic Citation Format

## DOCUMENTING SOURCES ON NOTE CARDS

From the beginning of the research process, all materials used must be documented. The following data on each source can be collected on note cards, accumulated, and used to prepare the Works Cited section after the rough draft is completed.

### Books

Name of author/authors or editor/editors

Title of book

City in which publisher is located (include state if city is not well known)

Name of publisher

Date of publication

Volume number if multivolume work

### Articles in Periodicals (magazines, newspapers, and journals)

Name of author/authors

Title of article

Title of periodical in which article appeared

Volume number

Date of publication

Page numbers

### Electronic Sources

Name of author/authors or editor/editors (if published)

Title of material accessed

Date of material (if provided)

Title of database or file used

Source type (online or CD-ROM)

Name of computer service if online (America Online, Prodigy, Internet, etc.)

Date of access (date material was retrieved)

## COMPILING WORKS CITED (ALSO CALLED BIBLIOGRAPHY)

After the rough draft of a paper is completed, the Works Cited section should be compiled. Citing the materials used in the paper gives credit to the authors and lets the reader know where the information was obtained. Gather note cards on which bibliographic data have been collected from all sources used during the research process. Arrange the cards in alphabetical order by author's last name. If the author's name is unknown, use the first word in the title (excluding *a*, *an*, and *the*) instead. Now the Works Cited section can be prepared.

Works cited can be arranged using many different formats, including Modern Language Association (MLA), Turabian, and *Chicago Manual of Style*. There is no need for confusion over which form to use, however, if two important points are remembered. First, always consult with the teacher who assigned the project to learn his or her preferred method of citation; then adhere to that system. Second, when choosing the method of bibliographic citation yourself, be consistent, use one source only, and follow the rules. These rules are published in books and pamphlets available at all libraries and school media centers.

## EXAMPLES OF MLA BIBLIOGRAPHIC FORMAT

Because MLA format has become standard in many secondary school systems, examples of format to be used in the Works Cited section of a research paper will conform to that style. As indicated above, there are alternative styles of format available.

### Books with One Author

Hauser, Pierre N. *Illegal Aliens*. New York: Chelsea House, 1994.

### Books with Two or Three Authors

Schemel, Sidney, and M. William Krasilovsky. *This Business of Music*. New
    York: Billboard, 1985.

### Books with Four or More Authors

Bankhead, Elizabeth, et al. *Write It: A Guide for Research*. Englewood, CO:
    Libraries Unlimited, 1988.

### Books with an Editor

Knappman, Edward W., ed. *Great American Trials*. Detroit: Visible Ink, 1994.

### Multivolume Work with an Editor

Trosky, Susan M., ed. "Maya Angelou, 1928–  ." *Contemporary Authors New
    Revision Series*,  Vol. 42. Detroit: Gale, 1994.

### Newspaper Article with Author

Zuckerman, Laurence. "With Internet Cachet, Not Profit, a New Stock Amazes
    Wall Street." *New York Times* 10 Aug. 1995, nat'l. ed.: C2+.

### Newspaper Article without Author

"How about Bosnia's Borders." *Wall Street Journal* 15 Aug. 1995, east. ed.: A16.

### NewsBank Article (or any microform collection of articles)

Brovsky, Cindy. "Gangs in Greeley." *Greeley* (CO) *Daily Tribune* 4 June 1995.
    *NewsBank*: *Social Relations* XXVI (1995): fiche 39, grids C9–10.

### Magazine Article with Author

Lemonick, Michael D. "The Last Frontier." *Time* 14 Aug. 1995: 52–60.

### Magazine Article without Author

"A Better Way to Manage Smog." *Science News* 5 Aug. 1995: 92.

### Magazine and Newspaper Articles Reprinted in Looseleaf Collection

Schraf, Joannie M. "Pumped Up." *U.S. News and World Report* 1 June 1992: 54+.
    *Drugs*. Eleanor C. Goldstein, ed. Vol. 5. Boca Raton: *SIRS*, 1990–1993.
    Art 52.

### Pamphlet (treat as a book)

Pines, Maya, ed. *From Egg to Adult*. Bethesda, MD: Howard Hughes Medical
Inst., 1992.

### Encyclopedia Article with Author

Likens, Gene E. "Acid Rain." *The World Book Encyclopedia*. 1995.

### Encyclopedia Article without Author

"Greenhouse Effect." *The New Encyclopaedia Britannica: Micropaedia*, 18th ed.,
1993.

### Electronic Sources

Consult an MLA or other style manual for citation examples covering
the many electronic information sources available. Following is the MLA
format for several commonly found sources in libraries.

### CD-ROM Periodical (Magazine and Newspaper) Index

Huffstutter, P. J. "Music Wants to Be Free on the Cyberspace Frontier." *San Diego
Union-Tribune* 14 May 1955: E1. *CD NewsBank Comprehensive*. CD-
ROM. July 1995.

### CD-ROM Encyclopedia Article

"Aids." *Grolier Multimedia Encyclopedia*. CD-ROM. Danbury, CT: Grolier,
1995.

### CD-ROM Reference Book Article

"King, Stephen." *Discovering Authors*. Vers 1.2. CD-ROM. Detroit: Gale, 1995.

### Online Sources

When citing material found in online sources, format as you would
printed material and add a reference to the source or service at the end of
the citation. For details concerning online source citation, consult a teacher
or librarian, or use a guide such as the following:

Li, Xia, and Nancy B. Crane. *Electronic Style*. Westport: Meckler, 1993.

# Appendix C: Guide to Searching Databases

Most school media centers and public libraries are equipped with a selection of CD-ROM computer databases that can be searched by subject to retrieve information on a wide variety of topics. Increasing numbers of libraries also provide access to online computer databases.

## WHAT IS A COMPUTER DATABASE?

A computer database is an electronic file of information. The type of information varies depending on the database. Some databases contain one or more of the following: the complete works of Shakespeare, the *Encyclopedia Americana*, multiple volumes of *Readers' Guide to Periodical Literature*, an index to thousands of newspaper and magazine articles, full-text (complete) articles from several hundred national newspapers, and many other kinds of information both specialized and general.

### CD-ROM Databases

Some familiar databases to library users are Grolier's Multimedia Encyclopedia, InfoTrac, EBSCO Magazine Article Summaries, WILSONDISC, CD NewsBank, Business ProQuest, and SIRS (Social Issues Resources Series). These are referred to as CD-ROM products because in each case the information is stored on CDs and played on CD-ROM drives. The CD-ROMs are updated periodically. These databases are usually provided by libraries as a free service, although there may be a charge for printouts.

### Online Databases

Online databases found in some libraries include Dialog, America Online, Prodigy, and Wilsonline. These services allow the user, through the library computer modem, to access information in computer files located outside the library. Generally, online databases are frequently updated and can be expensive. Costs vary considerably, though, depending on the database in use, the skill of the searcher, and the time consumed in searching. Librarians often perform online database searches for the patron and may charge a fee. Inquire about online services at your school media center or public library.

### Internet

A third type of database becoming popular in homes, schools, and libraries is the Internet. For those interested in learning more, many books and articles are available. For the purpose of this guide, it is important to understand that the Internet is composed of thousands of computers, computer networks, and databases located throughout the world. Information on almost any topic imaginable is available by accessing this immense and complex network. However, there is no governing authority to organize the vast amount of material into a system that allows for easy retrieval. Furthermore, there is often no way to guarantee the accuracy or currency of information that is obtained from Internet sources. Consequently, the Internet is considered a new frontier and those interested in exploring it will find it a fascinating, sometimes difficult challenge.

### WHY SEARCH COMPUTER DATABASES?

There are many excellent reasons to use computer databases as part of the research process. They enable the user to

- Search thousands of periodicals for information on a particular subject in a matter of minutes. The search can result in a list of bibliographic citations to articles, abstracts, or full-text articles depending upon the database product in use.
- Retrieve printouts of articles, charts, and maps on any one of a multitude of topics, from a CD-ROM encyclopedia without turning a page.
- Gather articles from newspapers around the country, even though the library subscribes only to several area papers.

- Access current information, even up-to-the-minute information for many online databases, from diverse fields of study that is not yet available in published format.

- Retrieve information on obscure topics available only in highly specialized sources not found in print format in most libraries.

- Search for information from multiple sources using variations of a subject heading or alternative terms, instead of using only one term as in a printed index.

## HOW TO SEARCH COMPUTER DATABASES

Each computer database is unique and has its own specific rules for effective searching. Before using any computer reference tool for the first time, it is advisable to request a demonstration by a librarian or at least read instructions posted near the machine. However, there are some general guidelines applicable to many systems. An understanding of these concepts will assist the user in operating most of the databases found in school media centers and public libraries.

### Focus on a Subject

Databases are accessed by subject, so it is essential to have a specific topic in mind before attempting the search process. Use dictionaries, encyclopedias, or any other pertinent reference source to identify the subject to be researched. Keep in mind that names are usually treated as subjects and often need to be entered last name first.

Attempt to narrow the subject. This is important because too broad a topic will retrieve an overwhelming amount of information and result in an unfocused, ineffective research paper. Some databases themselves provide subheadings to assist with the narrowing process. Use of the Research Topic Guides or consultation with a teacher or librarian can also help to narrow a topic.

### Select an Appropriate Database

Select a database appropriate for the research topic. Articles on genetic engineering will be available on InfoTrac and EBSCO Magazine Article Summaries but not on Biography Index. Similarly, newspaper articles covering the end of the Cold War can be located using NewsBank or other newspaper indexes but will not be found in a CD-ROM encyclopedia or in a magazine index. For books on the civil rights movement, use a database that contains books such as a computer card catalog. Magazine indexes like InfoTrac and WILSONDISC include only articles in periodicals, not books.

When in doubt as to which product to use, consult a librarian or read instructions posted near the equipment.

### Identify Terms

Information in computer databases is organized similarly to information in libraries. Each topic is assigned one or more subject terms (just as each book is assigned subject headings). These terms vary among databases but are often referred to as subject headings, key words, descriptors, or designators.

A successful database search depends on choosing subject terms that the system in use will recognize. In addition, the vocabulary used to search one database may not work in another. Prepare to search a database by making a list of terms that match or describe your subject. Following are suggestions for selecting subject terms:

- Some databases provide a thesaurus of terms used, either in book form or onscreen. Check to see if this option is available.
- Certain databases present onscreen an alphabetical index of subject headings and subheadings that can be directly accessed to retrieve pertinent information.
- Indexes in general encyclopedias, subject encyclopedias, and many books provide a wealth of terms that can be used to search databases.
- Experiment by using various forms of root words and creating plurals.
- Consider synonyms and related terms.
- Consult the *Library of Congress Subject Headings*, a reference source that lists all standard subject headings and subheadings used in most library catalogs. Many databases use these same subject terms.
- Consult *Sears List of Subject Headings* available in many libraries.
- Talk with a librarian or teacher who may suggest alternative headings to try.
- When using a Research Topic Guide from this book, try the recommended subject headings and key words listed.

### Develop a Search Strategy

A search strategy can be simple or complex depending on the subject involved and the database in use. Often online computer searches are more difficult for the novice to negotiate, mainly due to the large number of files or choices from which to select. Consequently, trained librarians may perform the search after discussing the specific information need with the patron.

CD-ROM database search strategies can be developed and performed by the user. Although specific instructions vary among products, certain guidelines can be applied to most database searches. CD-ROM computer databases usually offer at least two levels of searching.

*Level One Searching.* Often the first, and easiest, level is all that will be necessary to obtain required information. Level one searching involves entering a subject term or phrase (*ozone* or *green house effect*) and retrieving a list of citations to articles or the full-text articles themselves. These can be printed out in minutes (you will need to ask for the periodical if full-text is not available), taken home, and along with other material incorporated into a research paper. Sometimes a term or phrase fails to elicit results. Try another subject term or descriptor from your list of terms. This approach will be effective for many research topics.

*Level Two Searching.* If trying terms and descriptors from your list produces few results, a deeper level of searching will be required. CD-ROM databases allow the user to tailor a search in a variety of ways. Again, the specific rules vary among databases but the following techniques can be employed successfully in level two searching:

- *Truncation* is a technique used to search for words with plurals and multiple endings. This is often necessary because computers are literal and can search only for exactly what is entered. If the phrase *sex education* is searched, articles using any other form of the word *education* will not be found. But by entering a root word and symbol, such as *educat\** (the symbol will vary among different systems), the computer will search for words beginning with the root but having a variety of endings, for example, *educate, educates, educated, education, educational, educator,* or *educators.* Using truncation to retrieve variations of a root word allows the user to locate a greater number of articles on a topic.

- *Boolean searching* is a technique used to design a search to retrieve only the articles exactly pertinent to the research topic. The use of *and, not,* and *or,* known as Boolean operators, allows for further defining the terms of a search. Use these operators to connect concepts in a search statement. For example, entering the words *dogs and cats* will result in articles that include references to both dogs and cats. Entering *dogs or cats* will result in articles on dogs, articles on cats, and articles on both dogs and cats. Entering *dogs not cats* will result only in articles on dogs. Using *and* and *not* narrows a search and retrieves fewer articles, whereas using *or* broadens it to include more articles.

- This is a simplified introduction to Boolean logic, which can become complex when applied to more than two terms along with the use of truncation. However, most CD-ROM systems provide a preformatted screen that guides the user through a Boolean search.

There are additional techniques to aid in searching CD-ROM databases. These can be learned as needed in conjunction with the searching guidelines of a specific database.

# Appendix D: Research Topic Guide Template

# TOPIC

**BACKGROUND**

**BROWSE FOR BOOKS ON THE SHELF USING THESE CALL NUMBERS**

**LOOK UNDER THE FOLLOWING SUBJECTS IN THE CATALOG (CARD OR COMPUTER)**

**USE PAMPHLET FILE (ALSO CALLED VERTICAL FILE) UNDER THE HEADINGS**

**REFERENCE MATERIALS THAT MAY HELP (BOOKS OR CD-ROMS)**

**PERIODICAL INDEXES TO SEARCH (BOOKS OR CD-ROMS)**

**ONLINE DATABASES TO SEARCH**

**KEY WORDS AND DESCRIPTORS FOR PERIODICAL INDEX AND ONLINE SEARCHES**

**VIDEOTAPES ON THIS TOPIC**

**FICTION BOOKS RELATING TO TOPIC**

**NATIONAL ORGANIZATIONS TO CONTACT FOR ADDITIONAL INFORMATION**

**SUGGESTIONS FOR NARROWING THIS TOPIC**

**SUGGESTIONS FOR RELATED TOPICS**

This RESEARCH TOPIC GUIDE is intended to help the library user find information and materials on a particular topic in many sources throughout the library. Resources on this topic are not limited to those described and availability will depend upon the individual library. Feel free to ask a librarian for assistance.

# Bibliography

Anthony, Susan C. *Facts Plus: An Almanac of Essential Information*. Anchorage: Instructional Resources, 1991.

Bankhead, Elizabeth, Carol Marinez, Janet Nichols, and Ruth Anne Windmiller. *Write It: A Guide for Research*. Eaglewood, CO: Libraries Unlimited, 1988.

Baugh, Sue L. *How to Write Term Papers and Reports*. Lincolnwood, IL: VGM Career Horizons, 1992.

Berry, Margaret A., and Patricia S. Morris. *Stepping into Research!* West Nyak: Center for Applied Research in Education, 1990.

Everhart, Nancy. *How to Write a Term Paper*. New York: Franklin Watts, 1994.

Felknor, Bruce L. *How to Look Things up and Find Things Out*. New York: Morrow, 1988.

Gibaldi, Joseph. *MLA Handbook for Writers of Research Papers*. New York: MLA, 1995.

Hochman, Stanley, and Eleanor Hochman. *A Dictionary of Contemporary American History: 1945 to the Present*. New York: McGraw-Hill, 1993.

Katz, William. *Your Library: A Reference Guide*. New York: Holt, Rinehart & Winston, 1979.

Kuhlthau, Carol Collier. *Teaching the Library Research Process*. Metuchen, NJ: Scarecrow Press, 1994.

Li, Xia, and Nancy B. Crane. *Electronic Style*. Westport: Meckler, 1993.

Magill, Frank N., ed. *Great Events from History: American Series*. Englewood Cliffs, NJ: Salem, 1975.

Mann, Thomas. *A Guide to Library Research Methods*. New York: Oxford University Press, 1987.

*McGraw-Hill Encyclopedia of Science & Technology*. New York: McGraw-Hill, 1992.

Neff, Glenda Tennant. *The Writer's Essential Desk Reference.* Cincinnati: Writer's Digest Books, 1991.

*The New Book of Popular Science.* Danbury, CT: Grolier, 1992.

Peterson, Linda. *Starting Out, Starting Over: Finding the Work That's Waiting for You.* Palo Alto, CA: Davies-Black, 1995.

Phipps, Rita. *The Successful Student's Handbook: A Step-by-Step Guide to Study, Reading, and Thinking Skills.* Seattle: University of Washington Press, 1983.

Van Doren, Charles, ed. *Webster's American Biographies.* Springfield, MA: Merriam, 1974.

Williams, Michael W., ed. *The African American Encyclopedia.* New York: Marshall Cavendish, 1993.

*WILSONDISC CD-ROM Retrieval System: Quick Reference Guide.* New York: H. W. Wilson, 1995.

*The World Book Encyclopedia,* 1995.

# Index

## About the Author

BARBARA WOOD BORNE is reference and young adult librarian at the Wallingford, Connecticut Public Library, where she developed the prototypes for these research guides to help students with the research process. Before becoming a librarian she was a teacher in New Jersey, Indiana, and Connecticut, and an academic advisor at Michigan State University.